DEATH OF THE DREAM

DEATH OF THE DREAM

Classic Minnesota Farmhouses

WILLIAM G. GABLER

Afton Historical Society Press
Afton, Minnesota

Half title page: 1890s farmhouse kitchen, Minnesota Historical Society

Frontispiece: Lac qui Parle County family and guests at dinner, ca. 1890s, Minnesota Historical Society

p. 10: A three part L house in Maxwell Township, Lac qui Parle County,
photographed in 1898, Minnesota Historical Society

Designed by Barbara J. Arney

Sarah P. Rubinstein edited the text for this book.

The author wishes to acknowledge the assistance of:
Mary Meihack, fieldwork
Mary Carol Wagner, text preparation

Library of Congress Card Cataloging-in-Publication Data

Gabler, William G.
    Death of the Dream: Classic Minnesota Farmhouses/William G.
Gabler.
      p. cm.
    Includes index.
    ISBN 1-890434-00-0
    1. Farmhouses--Minnesota--Pictorial works.   2. Vernacular
Architecture--Minnesota--Pictorial works.   I. Title.

NA8208.52.M6G3 1997
728' .6' 09776--dc21   97-9503
                                         CIP

Printed and bound in Canada

The Afton Historical Society Press is a non-profit organization that takes
great pride and pleasure in publishing fine books on Minnesota subjects.

W. Duncan MacMillan   Patricia Condon Johnston
president   publisher

Afton Historical Society Press
P.O Box 100
Afton, MN 55001
1-800-436-8443

Then give me but my homestead
I'll ask no palace dome
For I can live a happy life
With those I love at home

— from a child's composition book lying in the refuse

CONTENTS

THE DREAM 11

THE STRUCTURES IN THE FIELD 23

THE PLATES 39

THE DREAM

IN THE NINETEENTH CENTURY many poor and disadvantaged persons had a common dream—to own their own land. They longed to work with their hands and to derive the benefit of their work free from exploitation and oppression. They wanted to farm, and they wanted to raise a family. The opening of the American West made it possible to realize that dream.

The farms that grew up on the prairie were humble and inglorious to look at, but they were high-output food-production operations, and the way of life of those first industrialized farmers gave the nation much of its economic might and many of its characteristic values. Now the basis for that accomplishment—the family farm—is disappearing from the land, and the structures of that life— the houses, barns, small towns, and railroads—are vanishing, too.

In the 1860s the forefront of the industrial revolution moved onto American soil where, for the first time, it demonstrated its power to unleash the independent productivity of the common man by providing the complex machinery of farming and railroading at affordable prices through mass production. That machinery made it possible for small family groups to farm profitably large pieces of land situated far from the regions of dense population in the eastern United States and Europe. At the same time machinery and transportation became affordable, the United States government made available millions of acres of free land, which attracted thousands of European immigrants to the American Midwest.

The closed societies of Europe yielded their excess population, which they were unable to integrate into their societies except as oppressed labor,

to the United States where the young open structure of American society offered the immigrant farmer an extraordinary opportunity. He could obtain not only free land of high fertility but also high prices for the produce of that land. The only requirements were good health and the will to work out a new life in a new land. The settlers on the Minnesota prairie took up that challenge and in the course of the hard work of settlement produced many thousands of plain and simple farmhouses whose unpretentious utility bespoke the classic virtues of pioneer life. The rigorous disci-

THE FEDERAL GOVERNMENT enlisted private enterprise to speed the distribution of Upper Midwestern land by granting millions of acres to railroads that advertised land for sale. *The Cultivator and Country Gentleman,* Albany, N.Y. January 18, 1883.

pline and unavoidable originality of pioneer life created a classic style of architecture—one whose forms embodied the essential methods and values used by a new mixture of peoples applying innovative technology in an undeveloped environment in the production of expanding economic power. An unusually high concentration of those now abandoned classic farmsteads occurs in the vicinity of Yellow Medicine and Lac qui Parle Counties in west-central Minnesota near the South Dakota border. There Norwegian, Swedish, and German settlers created a local expression of the industrialization of the American economy.

The immigrant farmers of western Minnesota were part of an advancing wave of settlement whose leading edge broke the virgin prairie to grow wheat to mill into flour to make bread—the very foundation of western civilization. Wheat growing began in the Middle East and moved westward across the earth, usually in the company of the most advanced technology of the day. When it arrived on the prairies of the American Midwest, it brought with it the first mass produced industrial machinery ever to be applied to virgin lands by free common people. The route taken by that advance of wheat cultivation into Minnesota may be traced back eastward through Wisconsin, Illinois, Ohio, Pennsylvania, New York, and then across the Atlantic to Europe. There it leads back deeper in time to the Mediterranean empires of Rome and Greece, to the kingdoms of Egypt, to the ancient city states of Mesopotamia, and finally to the Neolithic villages of the very first farmers of ten thousand years ago. In all that teeming history there was no nation whose farmers could even begin to match the output of the American pioneers on the prairie.

AMERICA'S CLASSIC INDUSTRIAL AGE

The industrial power and productivity of the United States compounded swiftly between the Revolution and the Civil War. Rapid technological evolution provided industry with the capacity to exploit the resources of the land, while rapid natural population growth and immigration supplied the labor. Pittsburgh and Cincinnati became the centers of the iron industry at the heart of heavy machinery production. They built the steamboats that coursed up and down the Ohio/Mississippi/Missouri River system as well as locomotives, rails, and stationary steam engines for mines and factories. The great success of the industrial North threatened the slave-power economy of the South, resulting in the Civil War, which made the government a major consumer of the same grain, meat, and lumber that found ready markets in the eastern United States and abroad. Immediately after the war the economic growth and expansion of industry in the Upper Mississippi Valley entered its great phase. The westward-advancing industrial development crested in Chicago between 1862 and 1893 during the period of the settlement of the western and northern prairies.

A cycle of classic American culture characterized by swift technical advance, wide individual opportunity, and efficient social organization developed between 1862 and 1893. The great steel industries forged millions of tons of high-quality, low-cost steel rails, which were driven westward to link the resources of the West with the markets of the East. The railroads carried out the wealth of the forests, wheat lands, iron ranges, and cattle ranches to the packing plants, mills, and factories in the cities on the rivers flowing out of the forests and prairies. Mail-order houses and department stores were estab-

lished to provide everyone access to the proliferation of products while the first skyscrapers were being raised to concentrate business offices near the trading activity. Rapid communications, thanks to cheap paper, high speed presses, coordinated news gathering services, and the telegraph and telephone, gave this expanding industrial organism a swiftly responsive nervous system that kept its individual cells, its citizens, in constant touch with the whole body of the nation.

In nineteenth-century America great challenge coexisted with great reward, which invigorated the individual citizen as well as the business and institution, and there was power to be gained from honesty and ability as well as exploitative opportunism and manipulative speculation. The culture was old enough to have sophisticated vices and young enough to have faith in the future, established enough to have abundant working capital, but still uncivilized enough to offer primitive geographical challenges, and that made this period in the history of the nation the one most able to assimilate wide-ranging individual abilities into the national well being. It is at this time that the nation seems to have had the best balance between its technical capabilities and its human values, which tend to be contradictory or at cross purposes with each other in many other periods of history. The simple and the sophisticated, the physical and the intellectual, the individual and the group, reason and passion, and art and science were all productively coordinated to a degree not matched since that time.

THE WHEAT BOOM

The industrial revolution in America fed on wheat. Wheat production was the object of much of the machinery of the new industries, and the wealth it created made it possible to generate secondary industries of luxury and convenience products and services, which were the basis for the con-

sumer economy that followed the classic production economy. The principal economic motivation that drove the settling of Illinois, Iowa, Wisconsin, and Minnesota was the high price of wheat in international markets. The price rose to about $1.55 a bushel (roughly eight times what it is today, allowing for inflation) in the years between 1853 and 1856, in part because Great Britain increased its purchase of United States wheat when the Crimean War cut off the shipping of wheat from the Ukraine via Odessa and across the Black Sea.

In the years between 1850 and 1860 wheat production in Illinois, Iowa, and Wisconsin quintupled. In Minnesota it gained international importance in

MINNESOTA WHEAT PRODUCTION	
1849	1,401 bushels
1859	2,186,993 bushels
1869	18,866,073 bushels
1879	34,601,030 bushels
1889	52,300,247 bushels
1899	95,278,660 bushels
	Source: U.S. Census

the years between 1860 and 1870. In that same decade the population of Minnesota rose from 172,000 to 439,000 and the number of farms from 18,000 to 46,500. That wave of economic expansion produced the classic family farms of western Minnesota and their characteristic farmhouses.

With the new wealth came new systems of trade and investment among those who handled the wheat. The ownership of the wheat usually passed to many different persons before the wheat was actually consumed. The farmer might sell his grain to a local mill or to a distant milling company, to the local elevator or to a major chain of elevators. Elevators could be privately owned or be corporations or cooperatives. Some elevators were owned by railroads, some by milling companies, and some acted like banks by extending credit to farmers against the value of their future harvests. Wheat was treated as an abstract commodity that could be moved about through time and space even before it existed because the farmer could sell the right to his wheat before he grew it. Large milling companies purchased many thousands of bushels for their storage supply, which they maintained to keep their mills grinding throughout the year, and they sometimes speculated with those stockpiles. Wheat brokers bought and sold wheat and the rights to future wheat in sometimes furious tumult in the wheat exchanges of Chicago, Buffalo, Minneapolis, St. Louis, and other midwestern cities. A complex and impassioned commercial culture grew up among the businessmen and financiers of Chicago and was recorded in novels such as *The Pit* by Frank Norris and *The Titan* by Theodore Dreiser.

CHICAGO: THE GREATEST CITY IN THE WORLD

Chicago became the greatest wheat market and the center of the most extensive railroad system in the world. The tracks radiated out from Chicago like a root system to absorb the wealth of the prairie. Trunk lines ran to Louisville, St. Louis, Kansas City, Omaha, Minneapolis and St. Paul, and Milwaukee. Branch lines went on to small cities and towns, integrating smaller railroads into the national system, and finally capillary lines grew into local areas to extract the riches of the forests, prairies, and plains and pump them back to Chicago. The meatpackers and wheat traders of Chicago evaluated, traded, and shipped the goods out of Chicago and on to Detroit, Cincinnati, Pittsburgh, and finally New York. Some goods were manufactured and returned to supply the

farmers and settlers with advanced machinery and building materials, and some went on beyond New York to supply the entire world.

Chicago pulsed and boomed with trading and transportation energy followed immediately by building and manufacturing. The energy of the city was enormous and heady with the excitement of making money and swept up in the rush of progress. As the surging locomotives converged on the city, they pushed up the first and greatest skyscrapers in the world to concentrate the sharpest and most powerful traders to direct and redirect the flow of goods and compound the power of commerce more swiftly, more efficiently, and more profitably.

International trade became so rigorous that the bankers of London had no choice but to learn to respect the wheat traders of Chicago, particularly because England had become dependent upon the United States for most of its imported wheat and beef. The Chicago Board of Trade was established to organize, regulate, and record the transactions of the exchange in wheat, corn, oats, barley, pork, beef, flour, and lumber. The office buildings of Chicago, and the private homes of the men who worked in them, represented the finest and most progressive architecture of the time.

MINNESOTA: THE GREATEST WHEAT REGION

In 1883 Minnesota became the greatest wheat-producing state in the United States, and Minneapolis became the leading flour-milling city in the world. Minneapolis was the home of the fastest, most advanced roller mills driven by the most efficient turbines set into the riverbed by the sharpest engineers of the time. Minneapolis mills produced the highest quality flour worldwide, and they milled the greatest quantity of it per year of any city anywhere in the world. The yearly output of one-hundred-

pound barrels of flour from Minneapolis mills rose from 2,052,840 in 1880–1881, to 7,434,098 in 1890–1891, to 14,863,395 in 1900–1901. The Minneapolis Chamber of Commerce was second only to the Chicago Board of Trade in the amount of wheat trading and financial activity conducted.

The men who created and applied this advanced technology and generated the wealth worked with intense effort and fierce competition in a social climate charged with exhilaration, pride, and a sense of potency and optimism. These people were not slaves to industry; they built it, ran it, and drove the forefront of human accomplishment ahead with it. These mills, factories, and railroads were not imposed upon the land by a few money-mad robber barons. They were complex, highly integrated production systems built and run by a great variety of individuals playing different parts within a collectively coordinated national economy. The enterprise was extremely efficient because these men were highly motivated to exert themselves by the opportunity to contribute directly to their society and to obtain tangible reward for their contributions.

The negative elements of human society, such as exploitation, oppression, crime, and injustice, were certainly present. Saloons and brothels proliferated in Chicago along with all the other businesses, and by the 1920s the city became a notorious center of organized crime. In the nineteenth century, however, crime was balanced in degree with opportunity so it did not consume the productivity of the nation.

DISPERSAL OF INDUSTRIAL ACTIVITY

The industrial energy was not confined to a few large cities. It was operating across the entire Upper Mississippi Valley on the farms and rivers and in towns and villages of all sizes. Towns like Eau Claire, Wisconsin, Dubuque, Iowa, and

Sioux Falls, South Dakota, built mills, factories, warehouses, and office buildings on the banks of their respective rivers. Steamboats and railways carried in the resources of the land to factories that both processed raw materials and built more machines for more factories. Then the finished products went out across the town wharves and through its railroad yards and depots. Now all those industrial structures are gone or converted to novelty shops and restaurants. The power and productivity of the original industries have dwindled and drained away, taking with it not only the prime motivating enterprise but the whole classic American culture as well.

In western Minnesota the industrial energy manifest itself in the expansion of the railroads, the introduction of lighter and tougher horse-drawn farm machinery, the use of steam tractors for threshing, and the proliferation of all sorts of tools and simple machines for use in the kitchen and the barnyard. All the mechanical means of farming became cheaper and more readily available, if not locally, then ordered via the rich and often beautiful mail-order catalogs. One could purchase everything from nails to steam engines from the unprecedented abundance of the Sears and Montgomery Ward catalogs. Nor were they only in the hardware business. You could buy eyeglasses, canned fruit, baseball uniforms, tombstones, and a great deal of information and vicarious experience via phonograph records, books, and photographs.

The great unsung accomplishment of nineteenth-century and early twentieth-century photographers (mostly American) documented the entire world and the industries of its peoples in stereoscopic views. Rural Americans of the nineteenth century had access to a more realistic and comprehensive body of world imagery than do present-day Americans. That imagery was encyclopedic in nature so each subject was objectively defined in terms of its physical appearance and its social position within the whole of world culture.

In Minnesota the Panic (depression) of 1873 stopped the expansion of the railroads just at the eastern edge of the western counties. Building resumed in about five years, which brought the tracks to Granite Falls in 1878 and on to Montevideo and Appleton in 1879. Another line reached Clarksfield in 1884.

By the middle 1880s all of the larger towns were linked by rail to each other and to the East. The railroad station became a gateway to the excitement and energy of all the people and products in the rest of the world. The railroads brought in lumber, machinery, livestock, mail, medicine, relatives, and salesmen. They carried out the produce of the land to the grain markets and stockyards of Minneapolis and St. Paul, Milwaukee, and Chicago. The small towns were in touch with each other via the railroad and the telegraph, and people used the railroad for personal trips and outings as well as long journeys eastward.

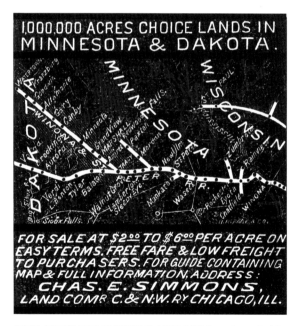

THE ADVANCE OF THE RAILROADS made profitable farming on the prairie possible. Freight depots for the railroad were established at fifteen mile intervals along the route and promoted the growth of new towns. *National Livestock Journal*, Chicago, Ill. September 1881.

SMALL TOWNS

Small towns were vigorous places in the 1870s and 1880s. They conducted the rudimentary business of the general store, the blacksmith shop, the livery stable, and the saloon as well as providing more complicated social services and entertainment. Hotels were profitable even in small towns because of the many people traveling through the West on business and personal trips. Almost every small town had its own bank. Unlike practically any other people in the world, Americans were genuine grass-roots capitalists who shared their resources by banking at the local level. Bankers knew everybody in their area, and persons who took out loans were generally careful not to overextend themselves and were conscientious about paying on time. For the most part daily business was conducted to the genuine satisfaction of both parties, and each transaction represented some sort of progress toward a promising future.

Most churches, fire departments, social clubs, and political organizations trace their roots to the formative 1880s. Each town had some sort of hall where dances were held and traveling entertainers put on shows. In the county seats, public buildings such as the school and the courthouse reached monumental proportions, dwarfing the rest of the town in a manner somewhat similar to the way medieval churches rose above their towns. Often these large structures grew up on the prairie even before trees were established on the town site, due to the rapid attainment of prosperity, making them appear somewhat out of place on the bare landscape.

PRODUCTION OF BUILDING MATERIAL

Industrial mass production manifest itself on the pioneer farm in the form of basic materials like shingles and lath, which the building boom of the latter nineteenth century devoured in large quantities. An average farm required about eighteen thousand shingles at about $3.00 per thousand and six thousand strips of lath at about $2.25 per thousand (Plate 21). In Minnesota there were approximately ninety-five thousand farms constructed during the building boom, which was part of the settling of the Midwest from 1862 to 1893. The same growth rate existed in at least eight other states until the onset of the Panic of 1893. By that time the pine forests of Minnesota and Wisconsin and the sawmills on the rivers leading from them had produced in the neighborhood of twenty billion shingles and ten billion strips of lath that ended up in farmhouses. Some sawmills specialized in high-speed production of those materials to meet the demand, and some mills could cut over half a million shingles a day in addition to about a million board feet of lumber. The total amount of lumber manufactured was around a quarter of a trillion board feet—a number quite beyond ordinary comprehension.

Such production was possible only with tough, ingeniously engineered, and beautifully designed machinery, operated by men who ran it hard and fast and without many breakdowns. The persons who designed the machines and the factory assembly lines, and those who coordinated industrial operations, were the ones most responsible for the high efficiency of American industry in the nineteenth century. Their machines were the true source of the new power because the machines did the work of so many men at once. Most of the other occupations provided fuel and raw materials for machines, operated machines, distributed the products of machines, or manipulated the wealth produced by machines.

The production of building materials in Minnesota was the western expression of a building boom present not only in the United States but also across Europe and in other emerging

nations, such as Canada and Australia. The United States generated the greatest amount of growth and building, however, which made the prairie farmers participants in one of the farthest reaching and most energetic expansions of human productivity in the entire history of civilization.

William H. Eldred,
MANUFACTURER AND WHOLESALE DEALER IN
SAWED SHINGLES
CAPACITY 300,000 PER DAY.
Can Load from 100 to 120 M Shingles in a Car.
OFFICE AND MILL,
Corner Sixth Ave. N. and River St., MINNEAPOLIS, MINN.
☞ SEND FOR PRICES.

INDUSTRIAL MACHINERY economically produced shingles, pickets, lath and all standard dimension boards and planks. *Mississippi Valley Lumberman and Manufacturer,* Minneapolis, Minn. October 27, 1876.

VICTORIAN ARCHITECTURE

Minnesota farmhouses were built within the Victorian period that included stylistic elements propagated by the Gothic Revival. This movement in turn was influenced by the anti-industrial philosophies of the Englishmen John Ruskin (1819–1900), William Morris (1834–1896), and August Welby Pugin (1812–1852), who sought to retain the traditional hand-crafted, preindustrial building techniques and styles of medieval England. So American industry propagated the decorative forms of an English anti-industrial philosophy.

The term Victorian implies an English origin for American architecture built during the reign of Queen Victoria (1837–1901), but Victorian architecture was, in fact, primarily a style far less prevalent in England than it was in the United States. Accordingly few examples of Victorian architecture may be found in England while thousands of examples may still be seen in the United States, and its pervasiveness may easily be traced through professional journals, such as the *American Architect*,

and the books and periodicals of the period. American architecture certainly used some English design elements, but they were compounded and synthesized into new forms for which no specific precedent may be found in England, and to imply that a major portion of nineteenth-century American architecture is essentially English denies the originating power and productivity of American culture, which was much greater than that of England at the time. English architecture and engineering influenced American architecture before 1865 while England was in the forefront of the industrial revolution, but when the United States gained primacy after 1865, it generated its own architecture of progressive originality.

THE ORIGINS OF THE FAMILY FARM

The farmhouses of western Minnesota were among the last structures created by the expansion of the American system of family farming, which began in 1607 and ended on the Dakota plains in the 1880s. The colonists at Jamestown in 1607 found that men without families and land of their own were not motivated to work the land. When women joined them and the colonists were allowed to own land, they took hold immediately and began to work the land with energy and tenacity. Farming families then forsook the security of the village and built their homes out on their land, spread apart from each other, which required each family to be responsible for its own welfare and to draw the necessities of life from within itself rather than depend upon the services of others. European farmers usually clustered in villages and walked out to their fields each day, while American farmers lived out in the midst of their fields and journeyed to the village for services and supplies. Harsh weather, accidents, and illness made living out on the land hazardous for independent families, but the desire to work their own land and to be physically close to it exceeded their fear of the dangers. Living with danger and uncertainty demanded individual strength. It obliged each individual to cooperate with other family members and each family to act in concert with its neighbors to manage events beyond the capacity of the individual or the family, such as defense against the Indians or more commonly the building of barns, roads, bridges, churches, and schoolhouses. These American pioneers developed an independent yet mutually supportive way of life in the wilderness. The frontier—the leading edge of the westward expansion—moved through New York and Pennsylvania in the 1700s, Ohio in 1800–1820, Indiana and Illinois in 1820–1840, Iowa and Wisconsin in 1840–1860, Minnesota in 1850–1870, and finally to the Dakotas, where the farmland ends and the range land begins, in the 1880s.

SUBSISTENCE AGRICULTURE IN MINNESOTA

The evolution of Euro-American agriculture in western Minnesota fell into three stages. The first stage extended from the passage of the Homestead Act of 1862 to the Panic of 1873. Those years formed the subsistence stage when the settlers established their presence and identified their essential survival systems and structures. Technology was based on ox power and hand harvesting and threshing with simple wood and iron implements. The basics of wheat production were mastered but not much excess was produced for the market. Life on the prairie was austere and so were the structures it depended upon. Buildings were gable-roofed sheds and lean-tos with only one or two rooms. Houses were built of sod, logs, or cheap lumber, few of which have survived. The essential structures of the successful farm were established, but it were not enlarged upon or refined in detail until later.

CLASSIC AGRICULTURE IN MINNESOTA

The classic stage, the stage of greatest originality and productivity, extended from the arrival of the railroads in 1874 to the Panic of 1893. During this stage the techniques, structures, and social systems of high-efficiency wheat production defined and established the classic styles and values of the region. The technology was based on horse-drawn iron and steel implements mass produced in the factories of the industrial cities. Those plows, seeders, cultivators, mowers, rakes, harvesters, and binders were built strong and light so they operated at horse speed, not the slower ox speed, and were efficiently adapted to the conditions of western wheat farming. A wealth of wheat flowed from the prairies to world markets via trains operating within social and commercial systems of highly integrated individual cooperation. The classic forms of houses, barns, grain elevators, railroad stations, storefronts, churches, schools, and courthouses were all generated at that time. The L-shaped and cube-shaped farmhouses reached their full development and became the architectural forms most representative of successful farm life on the prairie.

During these years American industrial development as a whole reached its classic phase and produced the most definitively American architecture both on the farms and in the towns. In the later 1880s and early 1890s wheat supply caught up with market demand and the initial soil fertility declined somewhat. The midwestern wheat boom ended, and specialized wheat farming moved on to California, Washington, and Oregon while midwestern farms settled back into more balanced general farming. Family farms diversified their operations to raise hay, corn, oats, barley, flax, cattle, hogs, poultry, and dairy cows along with their wheat. Farmers set about conventionalizing and politically institutionalizing the commercial and

social systems they had developed so methods and values that had been original and progressive became the established norm.

DISINTEGRATION OF AGRICULTURE IN MINNESOTA

The third stage was a long period of decline that extended from the Panic of 1893 through the Great Depression of the 1930s. During those years the strength of the family farm slowly eroded until the classic rural way of life effectively died.

In the years between 1893 and World War I, horses continued to be used for light work, such as cultivating, mowing, and pulling wagons, while steam tractors were used for heavy plowing and especially to drive threshing machines. After World War I and into the 1920s light and versatile gasoline tractors accompanied automobiles and trucks. Rural electrification began in the 1930s to bring convenient industrial energy into the kitchen and the barnyard, finally eliminating repetitive hand labor from the farm and with it much of the direct contact with the soil, plants, and animals.

Many farm structures built by the 1880s continued in use through the 1930s, and some have yet to be replaced. Some new types of buildings appeared, including tall silos, barns whose roof and wall formed one continuous arc, and sheet-metal pole barns. The latter were inexpensive to construct and non-monumental compared to classic barns.

After 1893 the classic L-house was no longer built except in degraded forms that lacked the balanced proportions of the principal room volumes and the delicacy of the open porches characteristic of the classic phase (Plates 27, 36). New farmhouses favored the cube form with front porches using Roman columns rather than Gothic pillars. They were followed by an assortment of city styles

ENGRAVINGS FROM THE 1860s depicted midwestern farm life to be most fruitful and harmonious. *The Prairie Farmer,* Chicago, Ill. 1864.

that did not represent the indigenous function of the farmhouse. Those forms included the bungalow, colonial, English cottage, rambler, ranch, and split level among many others.

After World War II the progressive originality of the national economy moved into the industries driven by the middle-class consumers of the suburbs, and the family farm lost its critical function in the American economy. Farming changed from a complete way of life to a defined occupation. Farmers began to employ overspecialized technology and overextended financing to produce one or two cash crops, usually corn and soybeans, using high-cost machinery and many chemicals on large acreages managed like corporate businesses. As the acreage per farm increased and the need for hand labor decreased the number of people living on the land also declined, and fewer farmhouses were needed. Several farms were combined to form one large farm, leaving one or two farmsteads unused except to house machinery in the old barns and sheds.

The farmers in western Minnesota in the 1990s, some of whom are direct descendants of the pioneers, are still independent, principled, and

courteous, but the old way of life has vanished. Fragments of families, such as a father and unmarried son or two bachelor brothers working together, manage the large farms.

Technological advances allow the contemporary farmer to work far more acres per year than could the nineteenth-century farmer, and the federal government has introduced numerous programs and subsidies designed to ensure that farmers have the same opportunity for success and security that is available to employees of the large corporations and institutions of the city, but federal measures have failed to stem the tide of people leaving the farms. The manipulation of capital and the exploitation of government programs have become so essential to farming that, it is said, many farmers no longer farm the land—they farm the bureaucracy.

PRAIRIE ECOSYSTEM

In geological terms the North American prairie of the nineteenth century was a young ecosystem whose boundaries and populations were in constant transition. The collective capabilities of the various species of grasses, wildflowers, legumes, and

rushes that made up the prairie gave it the capacity to carry on a constant struggle for territory with the forests to the east and the dry plains to the west. Most of the plant forms on the prairie were small, short-lived, and able to propagate quickly and expand into new territory that had been disrupted over time by glaciers and more recently by erosion, drought, and fire. Many grew in colonies composed of numerous individuals who persistently moved the colony across the prairie by sprouting new individuals from their spreading roots, so the colony was both mobile and long-lived even though the individual was neither.

The prairie grasses wove their roots together into a fibrous mat within the top three or four inches of soil, which enabled them to absorb most of the rainfall rapidly before it could seep down to the levels where the roots of trees and shrubs might use it. The grasses also were able to take in some precipitation directly through their leaves, never allowing it to reach to the ground at all. In order for the trees and shrubs to survive, the rainfall has to exceed the amount needed by the grasses or else someone has to eliminate the grass around the trees as was done for the windbreak trees planted in shelterbelts around farmhouses. Other factors, such as naturally occurring fire from lightning strikes, contributed to the dominance of prairie in areas where the rainfall amounts would support trees if they could once get established. Grasses grow their stems anew each year while trees and shrubs depend on the woody structure produced in previous years. If that structure is injured or destroyed regularly, such as by fire, the accumulative economy of the tree becomes ineffective relative to the annual economy of the grasses whose crowns are just below the soil level and are not destroyed by such agents as fire.

Depending upon rainfall, the prairie grasses grew to different heights in different parts of the country. Very tall grass grew in parts of Missouri and Illinois. There some species grew to twelve feet so, it was said, a man on horseback would disappear from sight upon entering a good stand of grass. Tall grass growing to about six feet covered much of Iowa, Minnesota, and the eastern portions of the Dakotas, Nebraska, and Kansas. Medium and short grass prairie prevailed all across the Great Plains to the west of the tall grass prairie zone.

The prairie in its entirety stretched from Ohio to Colorado and from Texas to Saskatchewan. The luxuriant profusion of prairie grasses and wildflowers dominated a vast area. It was a boundless collective organism that the prairie farmers supplanted with their domestic grasses of wheat and corn. The total area of prairie in Minnesota amounted to more than eighteen million acres, but so thorough have the farmers been that only about two thousand acres of prairie exist today, and less than ten acres of that is actual virgin prairie.

PRAIRIE FLORA

About 125 species of grass commonly grew on the prairie along with nearly a hundred species of wildflowers. A tropical rain forest, by comparison, may have far more different species of plants in one square mile than did the prairie in all of its hundreds of thousands of square miles. The prairie was not pure grass. Cactus, marsh plants, shrubs, vines, and brambles grew in scattered locations. Small woody plants that did well on the edge of the forest but not in the forest, such as the wild plum, raspberry, grape, prickly ash, and sumac,

flourished on the edge of the prairie where they sometimes overcame the grass and moved onto the prairie, allowing the forest to move in behind their colonies. The wild fruits provided the settlers with fresh fruit, which was otherwise rather limited on the Minnesota prairie. Farmers could grow currants, gooseberries, raspberries, strawberries, crab apples, and a few other nearly wild sorts of fruit, but in general northern prairie conditions were a little too harsh to allow for reliable fruit production, and successful orchards were limited to only a few favored locations.

The principal constituent of the sea of grass was big bluestem, which grew to a height of over six feet. Today big bluestem exists only in occasional patches and clumps in ditches and along railroad tracks. Other common grasses were little bluestem, buffalo grass, side oats gramma, Canada wild rye, wheat grass, switch grass, June grass, broom grass, green needle grass, cord grass, Indian grass, reed grass, and slough grass. There were also extensive areas of sedge and cattails, which resemble grass but do not have the jointed stems of true grasses. Some of the native grasses made good forage in their respective seasons, and the pioneers grazed their animals on them at first. Later the farmers steadily replaced the natural grasses with domestic hay crops of timothy, clover, and especially alfalfa.

The wildflowers included rose, coneflower, daisy, aster, morning glory, sunflower, goldenrod, phlox, gentian, and blazing star (Plate 7). They bloomed in successive waves from May to September and created expanses of radiant color

rarely seen today. Now the only wildflowers tough enough to dominate the available uncultivated acreage are yellow and white sweet clover, dandelions, tansy mustard, ragweed, spurge, and goldenrod. The prairie rose is still common in the ditches along the roads where it seems to thrive in spite of being cut back by mowing. Its heady fragrance is perhaps the most beautiful on the prairie. Enticing and complex like the domestic rose, but more spicy like the apple blossom to which it is related, the seductive scent goes straight to the heart— as though conscious reason and the body were utterly transparent.

No trees grew on the open prairie, but many were present in the river valleys, along streams, and beside lakes. The cottonwood, elm, green ash, and willow were the most common trees in western Minnesota. In more well-watered locations, especially in the Minnesota River Valley, burr oak, red oak, box elder, basswood, quaking aspen, and red cedar appeared in limited numbers.

The cottonwood is the largest tree that grows in prairie regions, and one of the very few living things on the prairie to reach monumental proportions. It may exceed ninety feet in height and have a trunk six feet in diameter. Pioneer farmers and ranchers used the cottonwood to build houses, barns, and corrals because it was the only wood available locally, but the wood is soft and brittle and rots rather quickly. It was not employed much in Minnesota after reasonably priced pine reached the western regions of the state in the 1870s.

Today none of the prairie land of Minnesota

looks like prairie, because there are groves of trees everywhere, but almost none of those millions of trees grew up naturally. Virtually all were planted and cultivated by farmers who suppressed the grass and favored the trees in order to protect their houses and barnyards from the wind (Plates 1, 40).

PRAIRIE FAUNA

The greatest animal on the prairie was the buffalo whose individual size and total population matched in animal life the vastness of the prairie's plant life (Plate 3). The buffalo was the largest land animal to live in North America since the extinction of the mammoths ten thousand years ago. A bull buffalo might reach a weight of three thousand pounds. The buffalo was a great, shaggy, ice-age mammal that was hunted by prehistoric humans thirty thousand years ago and by the Native Americans into the 1870s. Their numbers were estimated to be as many as sixty million, but they were reduced to the edge of extinction by white men in the course of about ten years between 1870 and 1880. They were shot by hide and meat hunters and by sportsmen from railroad cars.

The buffalo interfered with the railroad by blocking the tracks and by knocking down telegraph poles, which they liked to use as scratching posts. The telegraph company had sharp spikes driven into the poles to ward off the itchy bison, but the buffalo so enjoyed scratching against the spikes that they fought among themselves for the privilege and knocked down even more poles in the uproar.

Deer were common near the rivers as they are today, but the elk that existed in the nineteenth century are completely gone. Smaller mammals included the coyote, fox, raccoon, badger, groundhog, ground squirrel, fox squirrel, and the much disliked pocket gopher, whose mounds jammed up mowers and reapers.

Valuable furbearing mammals included muskrats in the marshes and some mink and otter along the streams. A few beaver survived into the twentieth century. Mice enjoyed great prosperity among the grass seeds, and jack rabbits and cottontails reached large numbers in some years, occasioning rabbit drives that sometimes yielded a thousand or more rabbits.

There were extensive wetlands on the northern prairie, in spite of the moderate rainfall, because the clay subsoil and the absence of a well-developed natural drainage network held the water on the land in thousands of little lakes and marshes. The irregular retreat of the glaciers left many holes and depressions scattered across the plain that filled every spring to provide nesting habitat for huge numbers of ducks and geese. The ancestor of the Minnesota River eroded a valley broader than the present river occupies, which left room for several lakes in the upper valley that now host one of the largest number of species of birds of any locality in the state. The great white pelican lives there in the summer, ignoring humans and continuing to execute the disciplined patterns of existence that evolved millions of years before the incursion of agriculture. They have knobby heads, long bills, and leathery pouches that make them look like pterodactyls. They are the largest birds in the state, with seven- to nine-foot wingspans that allow them to fly high with only a few wing beats per minute. They fly in precise formations, and they stroke their wings in unison so the whole formation flies as one bird. They also feed in formation. Six or eight get together shoulder to shoulder in shallow water and with their long bills dipped into the water they drive ahead in a row clattering and splashing their bills in front and kicking up a wake with their feet behind.

The great blue heron and the great white heron stride about in the shallows, stabbing at frogs and minnows, and there are cormorants along with

the ducks and geese. The principal upland game birds are the pheasant, introduced in 1905, and the hungarian partridge. Prairie chickens were common into the 1920s, but now have disappeared.

Many common songbirds live in western Minnesota although there are fewer species than in the more wooded regions to the east. The robin, flicker, killdeer, bluejay, mourning dove, crow, redheaded woodpecker, tree swallow, barn swallow, and blackbird are all present. The blackbirds, including the redwing and yellow headed sorts, are busy in the marshes in the spring, establishing individual territory and building nests. In the fall they rise up from their marshes and coalesce into flaring clouds of ten thousand and more to migrate. The gabbling and chattering of the blackbirds and the measured honking of the geese are some of the most common sounds of the region along with the rush and murmur of the wind and the swish of the grass.

ESTABLISHING THE FARM

The Homestead Act of 1862 made Minnesota land available for the asking. One could obtain 160 acres by paying a ten-dollar filing fee and then living on the land and farming it for five years. Since the land was free, the settler's money could be spent on other necessities, which enabled poor families who would otherwise be unable to make the journey to undertake the venture. Initial expenses were about $800 for a family of four. Besides paying for the trip to Minnesota, the settler had to buy lumber, hardware, stove, tools, food, and seed to build a primitive house and begin to carve out a self-sustaining existence, which cost about $160. The big-budget items needed as soon as location and shelter were established were a yoke of oxen for $150, a wagon for $100, a plow for $20, and a milk cow for $50. A start might be made for as little as $500, but that would require perhaps excessive dependence upon the help of neighbors, friends, or relatives. For about $3,000 a settler could travel comfortably, eat well, build a permanent house and barn, and buy a full set of basic livestock and machinery, but few homesteaders were that well capitalized.

The recipe for settling the West mixed together poor families with free land capable of producing crops of high value in world markets. The opportunity to obtain free land was extended to those who were not yet citizens of the United States, so immigrants faced no legal barrier to becoming land owners. Available land was taken up rather quickly, and the initial settlement of western Minnesota was essentially complete by the 1880s. In Chippewa County for example, there were thirteen hundred acres under cultivation in 1870 and forty thousand acres ten years later.

In addition to homesteading, there were several other ways for a settler to obtain free or reasonably priced land. Free land was available under the Timber Culture Act that required a claimant to plant a certain number of trees and to tend them for five years. Land also could be purchased from the government by real estate companies for about $1.25 an acre. It was then offered to the public by the agent at prices ranging from two to fifteen dollars an acre, and title to much of the finest land was transferred in that manner. The railroads, which had received land grants from the government, sold the parcels to the public for between two dollars and eight dollars per acre.

THE SHELTERBELT

In the beginning the farm might be in an area where not a single tree nor even a gully could be seen to interrupt the sea of grass or to provide the least shelter from the wind. The wind blows across the land at an average of twelve to fifteen miles per hour. It diminishes in the early morning hours,

but then it gradually picks up as the heat of the day builds. Most of the time it is not harsh or violently threatening, being, in fact, refreshing in the heat of high summer, but it is relentless and seems never to subside and allow a truly calm day. If the settler's mind was burdened with more trouble than he could see his way through, the persistent indifference of the wind might come to represent hopelessness. The farmwife was perhaps more subject to the strain of the wind because her homemaking was confined at first to a little house and a barren yard. The farmer at least moved about on the land as he struggled with the elements and achieved some feeling of control and confidence as he changed the face of the land in spite of the wind and weather.

RELIABLE AND REASONABLY PRICED PASSAGE across the Atlantic became available after the Civil War when a steady flow of immigrants began to settle on western Minnesota lands. *National Livestock Journal,* Chicago, Ill. March 1872.

The settlers fought against the emptiness and with their own hands gave new form to the prairie. They used common sense and transplanted the toughest native trees—the green ash, cottonwood, and elm—from the river valleys onto the prairie to form windbreaks to shelter the farmstead. Those shelterbelts could reduce winds of twenty to thirty miles per hour on the prairie to four or five miles per hour in the yard. Decreased wind speed in winter reduced heat loss from the farmhouse and barn and from the animals and people working in the yard. Since a protected animal required less food to generate heat than did one exposed to the wind, fuel costs and feed bills were reduced. The shelterbelt kept the yard free from gusting wind and snowdrifts, which formed in the lee of the shelterbelt, and not around the buildings (Plate 5). The slow melting of those drifts in the spring helped diminish flooding by giving the water more time to soak in rather than run off. The lessening of wind speed reduced soil erosion and airborne dust, especially when neighbors had good windbreaks whose influence overlapped, denying the wind any long uninterrupted runs. As the trees matured, some could be thinned out and used for fuel or fence posts. The trees gave the farm a measure of privacy at the same time they provided habitat for wildlife including game animals and many birds.

The state and federal governments encouraged the planting of trees. In 1871 the Minnesota legislature passed "An Act to Encourage the Planting and Growing of Timber and Shade Trees" that awarded farmers two dollars per acre per year for planting and nurturing trees. Congress passed and amended a series of timber culture acts between 1873 and 1877 that awarded 160 acres of land free to settlers who would establish trees on forty acres within five years. Farmers quickly learned from hard experience that tree culture required even more work than growing crops. The ground had to be broken and thoroughly cultivated a year before the trees were planted. Thousands of saplings had to be carefully planted four feet apart to allow for losses and thinning later which would ensure that the trees would be about twelve feet apart. They had to be clean-cultivated to keep weeds and grasses from robbing them of the limited moisture. A firebreak had to be plowed all around the planting to protect it from prairie fires. Livestock, chickens, and rabbits had to be kept away or they would chew up both the foliage and the stems of the tender little trees, and those were the more manageable difficulties. Drought, grasshoppers, or an especially cold or dry winter might still wipe out the whole planting. All these demands had to be met at the same time the farmer was desperately needed to break ground for the crops, build the house and barn, tend livestock, put up fence, and provide for his family. In spite of the best intentions, the farmer often neglected tree care to deal with other immediate needs, and the trees were overwhelmed by the prairie. If the trees failed, then the farmer's land claim was in jeopardy.

The tree acreage requirement was much too large. The act was also subject to legal abuse by speculators who filed numerous illegal claims in different areas and then sold the claims at a profit before the end of the five-year period when final title would be checked and verified. Honorable and experienced farmers and the members of the Minnesota State Forestry Association, formed in 1876, advised the federal government of the impracticality of the act and the abuse it engendered, which prompted Congress to amend the act. The government not only respected and accepted the advice of the farmers, it also printed their letters in the *National Forestry Report* so other prairie settlers might read about their specific experience. The amended act required only ten acres to be planted in trees and made allowances for unforeseeable losses due to grasshopper plague or fire or drought. The improved law resulted in

many trees being planted on the prairie, but it was always a tentative and imprecise legal instrument. The timber culture program was finally abolished in 1893.

THE FARMER

The farm functioned as an industry or complex of industries that rewarded the versatile individual who was capable of assuming broad responsibilities and making productive order out of the whole of life. The farm family could raise field crops, vegetables, fruit, and flowers as well as manage the wild trees and plants in its locality. The farmer worked with organisms ranging from two-thousand-pound bulls to birds and insects to yeast and bacteria, extracting from them meat, fat, eggs, seeds, milk, honey, fruit, leather, fur, feathers, leaves, roots, fibers, juice, wax, and bristles. As the farm became more mechanized, the farmer learned to operate seeders, cultivators, mowers, reapers, binders, pickers, pumps, engines, and transmissions and to use various new lubricants and tools that accompanied them. The Midwest farmer had to do the work of dozens of specialists. He was a nurseryman, veterinarian, carpenter, mechanic, blacksmith, plumber, roofer, painter, hunter, trapper, butcher, leather crafter, teacher, counselor, cowboy, teamster, engineer, business manager, accountant, entrepreneur, and administrator. He worked with soil, water, wood, wind, rock, iron, steel, concrete, leather, chemicals, paints, and explosives. He could use hundreds of hand tools, ranging from the shovels, hoes, forks, and rakes of the soil to the axes, saws, knives, and planes of woodworking to the hammers, files, drills, and wrenches of metal work, along with many special tools, like hoof cutters, ice saws, and spokeshaves.

Physical skill and mechanical invention were rewarded on the farm, and when men got together socially they enjoyed exchanging information about machines and methods they had used or

invented to make their work more productive. European visitors to the bonanza wheat farms of the Red River Valley were surprised at the extensive use of complex machines almost never seen in Europe. Not only were the Americans running big machines, but they also were always buying bigger machines. Small farmers took advantage of the turnover and bought good used machinery cheap, repaired it, and cycled it through their operations. Ultimately every farmer in the Midwest had a greater or lesser personal junkyard that supplied spare parts and looked like an ill-kept museum of technology.

THE FARMWIFE

The farmwife's sphere of responsibility was similar in magnitude to that of the farmer, but it had a different center. The farmwife created the physical and emotional environment of the home within the house. She guaranteed the maintenance of the proven survival systems while the farmer pondered new technology and inventions that might contribute to the success of the family. She managed the provision of food, clothes, warmth, and rest, and organized the house to be a secure base of operations for herself and her husband, for the bearing and rearing of children, and for the conducting of all physical and social operations internal to the family. Her stove fired the central glow of the life of the family, and her kitchen was the single most important place on the farm. The farmer's hopes and fears for the future were discussed at her kitchen table where most of the meals were served, where the children did their schoolwork, and where most of the cooking, canning, and sewing was done. All outsiders—visitors, tradesmen, neighbors, egg customers—had to deal with the central coordinator, the farmwife, because even if their business was strictly with the farmer he was often far away from the house in the fields.

If the flow of energy on the farm were likened to a musical composition then the farmer played the melody while the farmwife kept the rhythm and tended to the harmony. She cooked, canned, washed, cleaned, sewed and mended, and looked after all the needs of the children. She kept the gardens, raised chickens, gathered eggs, and tended bees. She carried out dozens of household chores without plumbing or electricity. She had a number of simple machines to help her, but every one of them had a lever or a crank or a treadle that she had to activate with her own power. Responsible for maintenance of most of the family's social relations with the church, school, and relatives, the farmwife might also keep the books and records of the farm and write most of its letters.

The farmwife maintained the unbroken flow of effort on the farm uninterrupted by vacations or extended leisure time. Rest and regeneration and amusement and delight were natural elements of farm life integrated into production and not separated from it or opposed to it. The farmwife's work was never done because the family aspired to accomplish more than it could actually complete at any given time, and even if the farmwife did get caught up, it wasn't for long. About the time she felt she was catching up, she would discover she was pregnant again, and the farmer would stride in and announce his new plan to buy more land and try a new crop. She was the first one up in the morning and the last one to bed at night and generally on call for any emergencies through the night as well.

She had fewer breaks in her routine than did the farmer, who had occasion to go to town on business or go see a neighbor to arrange for help or stop by the saloon to talk about weather, prices, and politics. The women were not as mobile as the men and were sometimes isolated on the farm, which caused them some loneliness and sense of oppression. They were partners in a demanding enterprise whose challenges brought out their strengths and obliged them to take charge of the household and run it rather than let it run them.

THE FARMWIFE AND THE WHEAT HARVEST

As the family's social coordinator and general facilitator of complex group activities, the farmwife managed most of the support services critical to harvesting and husking corn and threshing wheat, when machines and threshing crews went from farm to farm to get the wheat in while the weather was fair. The American wheat harvest was the greatest single agricultural event in the world at the time, and much extra effort was put forth to accomplish it on time. Thomas D. Isern, author of *Bull Threshers and Bindlestiffs*, discussed many aspects of the human vitality of the midwestern wheat harvest. Thousands of professional threshing crews followed the ripening wheat from Texas to Saskatchewan, staying at each farm for a few days of concentrated effort. The farmwife had to rise to maximum output to keep all hands fed and happy. The wheat harvest was a time of excitement because it demanded high performance under pressure. Farmwives claimed that they liked to see the threshers come and liked even more to see them leave. Some women dreaded the harvest because it overwhelmed them, but most dug in and applied the work systems and division of labor that they and their mothers had created as the American wheat industry grew.

The threshers burned up energy fast, requiring five meals a day. The farmwives competed with each other for the compliments of the threshers who praised the excellence of their cooking and were especially impressed when the high quality came in great quantity. Farmers often provided the best food they had to the threshers, realizing that the fastest and happiest crews got their wheat to market in the quickest and most profitable way.

In addition to cooking large meals, the farmwives would carry two of the five meals out to the field to serve to the crew. They also carried drinking water to the fields, rendered first aid at accidents, kept the children clear of the most dangerous machinery, and helped find sleeping accommodations for the threshers in a fresh part of the barn or granary. The threshers often were working many hundreds of miles away from their homes, and the farmwives took it upon themselves to look after them, often setting out wash basins and towels for freshening up before meals in the farmhouse so the grimy men did not start feeling completely uncivilized and to keep their kitchens from becoming dirty. The wheat traders of Chicago owed much to the humanizing care that the farmwife extended to the itinerant threshers.

Persons who worked with farm women on classic farms say that, in retrospect, they simply do not see how the women got so much done or when they got enough sleep. Successful farmwives were adroit family managers who wove together many different streams of effort and persistently maintained the unbroken flow of interaction with the environment. That unrelenting maintenance, no matter how bad things got, was both the curse and the glory of the life of the farmwife. When one reads the memoirs of farm women who lived through the hard times of the 1930s, for example, they often give sobering accounts of toil and trouble and fear and heartbreak, but they did get their families through, and they note, a little surprised at themselves, that those were the best years of their lives.

THE STRUCTURES IN THE FIELD

OBJECTIVE AND METHOD OF THE FIELDWORK

The object of the fieldwork for this project was to look at as many farmhouses as possible in the vicinity of the Minnesota River Valley and determine the predominant forms without preconceptions about their origins. The method of the fieldwork used in the research was to drive down every road in a given county and look at every farmhouse. In some regions all the east-west roads were driven but not all the north-south ones, or vice versa, because it was possible to look down the crossroads and determine the character of a house without driving right up to it. It was still necessary to drive down the crossroads whenever a nice old house was discovered on one or when a house was obscured by the trees of its shelterbelt. The residential and downtown streets in the towns and villages were also explored, but only those in the old parts of town that might be expected to have nineteenth-century architecture. The total number of miles driven was about sixty thousand and the total number of farmhouses observed was about twelve thousand. Some 250 of those were photographed, and thirty-six appear in this book.

COUNTIES STUDIED

The counties studied intensively were Yellow Medicine, Lac qui Parle, Big Stone, Chippewa, and Renville, all at the western end of the Mississippi River Valley. Additional counties in the valley were also investigated, including Traverse, Swift, Lincoln, Lyon, Redwood, Sibley, McLeod, Nicollet, Carver,

and Scott, but those counties were not driven as thoroughly as the first mentioned group because the concentration of classic architecture proved to be lower in them. At present the number of classic wooden L-houses diminishes in every direction away from Yellow Medicine and Lac qui Parle Counties, but classic L-houses and many sorts of variant L-houses may be found throughout the farmlands of Minnesota and in the agricultural regions of most of the rest of the nation as well as Canada.

The roads on the prairie are in good repair, and there are no wild or remote areas that they do not cross or at least enter. Before 1960 midwestern

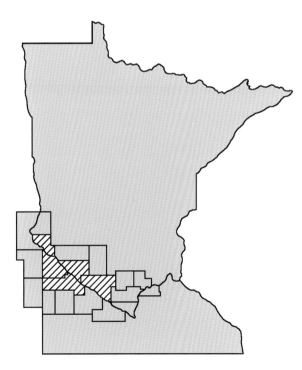

THE COUNTIES in the center of this group were most intensively investigated.

country roads had a peaceful natural energy around them that appeared irrepressibly good and potent, and the life of the country roads seemed divorced from the values and the pace of the cities. Now the country roads feel like extensions of the city that have forced the countryside to fall away before them. The roads and ditches have become wider, and the fields begin farther from the road. The shoulders and ditches are mowed and sprayed more regularly, so the grass and wildflowers rarely reach their full height and lean over the road as they once did.

ABANDONED FARMSTEADS

As a car turns off the township road onto the driveway of an abandoned farm, it seems to become a boat nosing through a rolling sea of grass. The yards, too, are deep with grass. If the barn and sheds are still being used to house machinery, then the yards are mowed and kept free of the old machinery, boards, wire, and tree limbs that litter completely abandoned yards (Plates 25, 44). Even the trashy yards are still clear of nails and glass, but there are occasional rocks and holes hidden by the grass. The principal dangers near the house are uncovered cisterns, hidden by the grass or snow, and rotten cellar stairs.

If the present owner of an abandoned farmstead lives nearby and sees a stranger on his land, he is likely to investigate. Farmers do not particularly resent photographers, but they are very interested in anyone setting up a tripod on their land because the photographer resembles a land surveyor who may be doing the groundwork for some future encroachment on the farmer's property. The farmer may also be made uneasy by persons who want to walk around in houses with rotting floors, falling ceilings, collapsing staircases, and broken glass lying all around, and the photographer has to be especially respectful of those houses that still contain some of the personal effects of previous occupants, which the farmer feels are best left alone to decay in peace.

The first impression conveyed by the old farmsteads is that they were plain and remote (Plates 12, 13). One wonders how the farm family could sustain itself, let alone feed a good portion of the rest of the world. The classic farm was a complicated enterprise whose success required careful management. When all living things are removed from the farm, it becomes difficult to see how it worked and what the product was, and interpreting farm life from the abandoned buildings is like trying to determine the daily behavior of an animal from its fossil skeleton.

THE ORDINARY FARMHOUSE

The typical nineteenth-century midwestern farmhouse was plain and unharmonious in design. It was quickly and expediently constructed and then expanded by adding on new rooms as needed and when income permitted. Most of them do not appear to be promising subjects for aesthetic analysis because cheapness, awkwardness, and downright ugliness seem widespread and even general (Plates 14, 23). At first one has the uneasy feeling that those who disparage farm life may be right, that the farm family was relegated to a coarse way of life because they were not bright or ambitious. Upon intensive study, however, the real way of life begins to be revealed, and when thousands of houses are examined within their surrounding yards and fields beautiful ones begin to stand out (Plates 17, 25). These houses were lived in by honest people who meant business and who succeeded or failed by their own efforts.

PRESENT APPEARANCE OF THE FARMHOUSES

Many of the houses have been left standing open, neither locked nor boarded up, allowing any creature full access to the interiors (Plates 21, 45). They are dismal. Some have taken on an air of mystery and threat. Windows are often broken, woodwork is torn out, ceiling plaster lies scattered across the floor over caked chicken and pigeon manure among dog droppings. The smell of old damp wood and decay is universal, giving the general impression of trashiness. Rags and cans and bottles lie among the folds of fallen wallpaper and heaps of newspapers and magazines (Plate 57). Shredded shades and rotten curtains hang in the windows, and barn swallows affix their nests above the door frames. In all but a very few cases, the original cupboards, tables, stoves, and sinks have been replaced long ago with cheap manufactured versions that confound the memory of the patterns of work that went on in the original kitchens. Some floors are covered with dirty, bald carpeting, others with linoleum, but most still wear their old dull-colored paint. Secondhand lumber, bags of cement and feed, storm windows and screens, and stoves and washing machines have been stored in some houses. A few houses have an entire end wall cut out to allow a combine to be driven in and parked in the living room. Most rooms are empty, and when furniture is found it is of the tacky contemporary sort, indicating that the last residents were situated well down the economic ladder. Often the last inhabitants had children whose broken toys and schoolbooks and work papers have been left behind on the bedroom floors. In a few instances the final occupants appear to have been counterculturists, who slept on mattresses on the floor, lived cheaply, and painted the bedroom walls in garish hues.

Discarded newspapers and magazines found on the floor usually date from the 1950s through the 1970s. They are mostly popular general magazines such as *Life, Look, Collier's, Saturday Evening Post, Time, Newsweek,* and *Reader's Digest.* Sears and Montgomery Ward catalogs from the 1960s and 1970s are common, and the farm journals most frequently subscribed to appear to have been *Successful Farming* followed by *The Farmer.* Newspapers subscribed to were typically local publications printed at the nearest medium-sized town rather than those of Minneapolis, St. Paul, or Sioux Falls, which are the nearest big cities. Religious periodicals, generally Lutheran, turn up about as often as farming periodicals—evidence of the religious affiliation of most families. Technical and practical pamphlets published by the U.S. Department of Agriculture are sometimes mixed in with the magazines. The business papers of the family also are at times found in the clutter. They include old income tax forms, canceled checks for fuel and groceries, receipts for grain, hogs, and milk, and an occasional postcard. Typically they are strewn on the floor among the rags with the shoebox sort of carton that they were kept in lying nearby.

The earliest records found in this research dated from 1888. They were the first entries in an account book owned by a farmer who may have been something of a dandy and a socialite. Among the usual entries for hogs, cream, and hay sold, were expenses for a new suit at $15.00, dress shoes at $2.50, collar buttons at $.35, violin strings at $.30, a songbook at $.80, and concert tickets at $.50. Those entries, along with regular repair entries for his sleigh and buggy, suggest that the farmer liked to dress up and get out socially with some frequency. Another accounting of monthly income and expenses in 1949 was recorded on the back of a notice from Senator Hubert H. Humphrey advising farmers that a pamphlet being introduced into the state was written by two persons who had held positions in Communist organizations. Such account books and records may fill in some of those portions of the farmer's spectrum of human behavior that cannot be precisely extrapolated from the bare buildings that remain.

Sometimes checks and receipts from the 1940s and 1950s are still tied together in chronological order, conveying an idea of the farmer's daily and weekly business with the feed store, grain elevator, gas station, and grocery store. It seems strange that such items are still in some of the houses after they have been lived in by successive families and tenants, finally abandoned, and then stripped of all parts with any tangible value. Apparently when the occupants of a farmhouse move out, they select only the articles of value among their possessions and leave the rest behind. When new tenants move in, they do not clean out every nook and cranny; they fit themselves into the situation they find. When the houses are vacant, vandals, perhaps in the form of children or hunters, enter and dig out all the old boxes and books and throw them onto the floor. In recently abandoned houses, even piles of good clean clothes, canned food, family snapshots, and fully decorated Christmas trees may be found simply left behind (Plate 66).

In many houses, the last inhabitants left calendars hanging on the wall, usually dating from the 1960s and 1970s. Farmers do not throw out a good calendar just because it is out of date; they put up a new one alongside of the old one, so six or eight calendars spanning twenty years or more may hang in the kitchen and living room. The earliest one found came from a Montevideo bank in 1947. On average these houses have probably been vacant for about twenty-five years with some abandoned thirty-five years ago or more. Some are in the process of being left because the movement off the land continues.

When a common farmhouse is abandoned, the contents of the rooms slowly disappear, and the weather moves in. First, the house absorbs moisture and becomes damp and rotten, which removes the paint, wallpaper, and plaster. Then air and light and heat enter through the broken windows and rotted roof to dry and bleach the boards until finally the house is cleaned to the bones, and it becomes stark and silent (Plate 20). The absence of architectural specialization and the plain simplicity of the structure belie the color and variety of the life that went on within it, and there is no remaining indication of the farm's vital role in the international economy of the nineteenth century.

DISPOSITION OF THE FARMSTEAD

The ideal site for the farmstead was on a broad, low hill or a gentle rise that would provide both good air and water drainage. Technically the most efficient location was in the center of the property so all the fields were equidistant from the barnyard, but that put the farmstead at the end of a long

MINNESOTA PRAIRIE LANDS were among the most rationally divided in the world. Township roads delineated one mile square sections, each usually containing four farms of 160 acres each. The farm fields are predominantly rectangular, and the shelterbelts of trees point toward the source of the winter winds to the northwest.

driveway, which tended to isolate the family from the society of the neighbors (Plate 68). Farmwives and farm children liked to be within sight of the road so they could be aware of the goings on of the neighborhood. Maximum sociability could be accomplished by locating the farmstead at the corner of the property, at the crossroads, but that meant that the outlying fields were quite a distance from the farmstead. Most farmers compromised and put the farmstead in the center of one side of the property with the house moderately close to the road, provided they had some high ground there.

The right of way for the road extended thirty-three feet from the center of the road onto the farmer's land, which provoked more or less continuous bickering and fussing about where fences should be, how ditches should be shaped, who paid for culverts, the placement of mailboxes, the number of trees allowed to grow in the ditch, who mowed or sprayed the ditch and when, and a number of other irritations. Farm families essentially cooperated with one another, but they were quick to rise up and debate the motives of those who would impose changes on any part of their land, even if those same persons were elected officials operating on their behalf, and even if there was an existing right of way.

The farm was divided laterally by fences to distinguish the various living areas and plant and animal production areas from each other. It also had some degree of vertical zoning, ranging from the aerial regions of the windmill, lightning rods, and hayloft to the subterranean realms of the root cellar, the cistern, and the bottom of the well (Plates 11, 50). In the early days the farms had few subdivisions because relatively few special operations were carried out and fencing materials were expensive or hard to find. After the farms became more thoroughly developed and cheap wire fencing became available in the 1870s, fences divided the farm into about ten different zones and areas.

The various areas and groups of areas fell into an approximate hierarchy of ever smaller spaces.

The farm was the sum total of all the land owned, including fields, pastures, meadows, wetlands, wastelands, roads, ditches, and the farmstead. The farmstead was all the land lying near the house. Within the farmstead lay the shelterbelt, the house yard, the barnyard, all the farm buildings, and the animal enclosures. The shelterbelt ran along the north and west sides of the farmstead as an area exclusively devoted to windbreak trees. The house yard was the area immediately around the house. The front yard extended from the formal front of the house to the county or township road (Plate 17). It contained a lawn, a flower garden, a vegetable garden up to about one-fourth acre in size, and possibly two or three fruit trees. The backyard had the clotheslines strung across it and also the outhouse. The house yard was often fenced to keep the chickens out of the flowers and vegetables. The barnyard served as an informal courtyard about 150 feet square in which practically every one of the farmer's chores began and ended (Plate 42). Wagons were loaded

and unloaded there by bringing out whatever was needed from the house or the barn or the tool shed to make up the particular expedition of the moment. There machinery was repaired, adjusted, sharpened, and lubricated. The horses were harnessed to the machinery in the barnyard, and when they were not working they might be groomed there. Cowyards, pigpens, and horse corrals were built between and behind buildings. Usually the axes of all the buildings were either parallel or at right angles to each other. The principles of farmstead organization were general, and the specific dimensions of each farm appear to have been unique, especially when the site was hilly. If the terrain was irregular, then all the buildings were constructed with much less regard for keeping their axes parallel or at right angles to each other.

THE BARN

The house and the barn were the two most important structures of the farmstead buildings, but neither one was either the geographic or the

THE FARM WAS A SELF-CONTAINED ENTITY, like an organism, with a definite shape. This house sits upon the highest rise in the farmstead island with its base appearing just above the tassel height of the surrounding cornfield.

activity center of the farm. The barn was usually placed diagonally across the barnyard from the house so the house and the barn tended to form the poles of the farmstead. The barn was the most monumental building on the farm because until the advent of the tractor, the farm ran on hay, and hay was bulky to store (Plates 10, 11). The bigger the barn the more horses, the more horses the more power, the more power the more acreage under cultivation, the more acreage under cultivation the more grain produced to sell or feed.

Farmers made hay during the summer while the other crops were growing. Hay could be made from various grasses and legumes, both wild and domestic. It was cut about three times a year, depending upon the rainfall. Cutting the hay and raking it into windrows to dry was done with horse-drawn equipment, so that part was not excessively strenuous, but then the hay had to be lifted onto the wagon with hand forks, which became increasingly difficult as the pile grew. Then the hay was carried to the barnyard, hoisted up into the barn, and stacked loose in the loft. The farmer might lift and stack up to a hundred tons of hay, which was long, hot, dusty work, but the result was a barn full to the rafters with the fodder needed to get the animals through the winter.

The gambrel-roofed, plank barn was the most common barn built on the prairie in the nineteenth century (Plate 10). It resembled the bank barns built by German farmers in Pennsylvania in the first half of the nineteenth century. The form was spread throughout the Upper Midwest, and in the eastern Minnesota River Valley, true bank barns built into a bank or hillside still exist. The bank barn allowed cows to walk in and out on the ground floor on the downhill side, while wagons could be drawn into the barn on the second floor on the uphill side (Plate 61). The soil around the barn stabilized the temperature of the barn somewhat, and the second floor served as a threshing area, although threshing above the cows tended to

drive chaff and dust down through the cracks in the floor and into the pails of fresh milk. On flat sites farmers sometimes built earth ramps to the second floor because they did not want to lose the use of it as a threshing floor, and they liked to be able to drive into the barn. By the time farmers in the west were building their barns, threshing machines were doing most of the work, and a hand-threshing floor was no longer needed. The second floor of most western barns stored just hay and could be reached only by a ladder (Plate 11).

The most common barn size was about thirty-four by forty feet with sixteen-foot side walls and flat end walls rising about thirty feet under a gambrel roof (Plate 10).

The roof was formed from four planes that rose in a high arch springing from the top of the side walls. In the ideal model, the lower planes of the roof were at sixty degrees to the horizontal and the upper planes were at thirty degrees to the horizontal, but like most farm structures, almost all barns appear to be variations on an ideal form, not replications of one. The lower edge of the roof kicked out at the eaves to throw water clear of the walls. It made the roof look a little like a traditional Dutch peasant woman's hat. The steep roof shed water fast and allowed more hay to be stored in the loft per square foot of floor space. The ground floor housed the horses and cows and might also be subdivided into stalls for pregnant animals or tool rooms and harness rooms before the farmer built special structures for those needs. The end wall facing the yard was fitted with a large hay door, about nine by fourteen feet, at the top of the wall under the peak of the roof (Plate 10). The roof was built out about six feet beyond the hay door, and the underside of the extended roof ridge carried a track that allowed hay to be gathered in a sling and hoisted up under the roof by horse-drawn rope and pulley and then rolled along, suspended from the track, into the barn and released wherever the stacker wanted it (Plate 11).

The barn walls were covered with pine siding and the roof with the same pine shingles as those used on the house and other outbuildings. All the materials used in barn construction were standard dimension lumber, identical to that used in the houses except that the pieces were wider. Barns were built of two-by-six-inch wall studs and roof rafters. The two-by-twelve-inch floor joists lay on eight-by-twelve-inch girders that rested in turn on eight-by-twelve-inch posts. Both girders and posts were built by spiking together four two-by-twelves. They were called plank barns because nothing larger than two-by-twelve-inch planks was needed to construct them. Earlier barns were built with a skeleton of solid timbers that carried the weight and resisted the wind. In the plank barn those pressures were spread more uniformly throughout the walls and roof so the entire structure absorbed the pressure.

OUTBUILDINGS

In addition to the barn, there were about six other buildings arranged around the barnyard, including a granary, hoghouse, henhouse, machine shop or tool shed, corn crib, and outhouse (Plate 42). The granary was a moderately tall, square building containing three or four internal bins formed by wooden partitions. The bins held corn, wheat, oats, barley, and later soybeans to be fed to the livestock. The height of the granary provided easy gravity feed of the grain through the little sliding door at the bottom of each bin. Most barns, grain bins, and corn cribs were tall compared to their modern counterparts. The height made them difficult to fill at the top but easy to unload at the bottom. Silos also were among the tallest gravity feed storage structures on the farm. They became common in the 1890s as practical technology evolved, and the farmer began growing crops suited to ensilage and keeping large numbers of cattle or hogs (Plate 65). Classic farms were in general oriented vertically compared to modern farms, which are typically low and spread out. The latter employ more engines and machines to move materials around laterally rather than relying on gravity to carry them down vertically. The windmill tower and the two-story farmhouse added to the verticality of the classic farm.

The hoghouse was located near the barn downwind from the house. The henhouse was usually placed an intermediate distance from the farmhouse and could be recognized by its many windows that provided the abundant light the chickens needed to regulate their daily activities and to stimulate steady egg laying. Windows were generally scarce on outbuildings because they made the structures more expensive, more difficult to build, and colder. Farming experts and authorities were forever harping at farmers to put more windows in their barns, but western grain farmers did not pay much attention because they did not have the large dairy herds that most benefited from well-lit barns.

The corn crib stored dry corn still on the cob. It had slat or wire sides to allow free air circulation to facilitate drying corn (Plate 42). Corn cribs were rather loosely constructed, which made them easy targets for raids by the fox squirrel whose habitat was enlarged when the farmer created shelterbelts and cultivated corn.

The machine shop was placed near the house and varied a great deal in size and complexity, depending upon the farmer's mechanical ability and zeal to control his operations. Some farmers had no machine shop and went to neighbors or to town for special repairs and services while others had complex shops and could repair or build practically anything needed on the farm.

The outhouse was the smallest of the outbuildings. It was not placed in the barnyard with the rest of the outbuildings, but rather between the house and the shelterbelt or in the first row of trees in the shelterbelt.

WELLS

The pump was perhaps the single most important piece of equipment in the barnyard, and much of the other equipment of the farm functioned around it. The pump was usually located about half way between the house and the barn so it could serve both animals and people (Plate 42). Ideally the well was dug on a little rise at least forty or fifty yards away from any animal wastes that might seep into it. Often it was on the perimeter of the barnyard, but sometimes it was in the middle with the driveway encircling it. Methods of water provision varied from one farm to the next as did most operations. Most drew water from one or more wells dug twenty to forty feet into the glacial till. Some had a well under the house for the kitchen pump although most of the time the kitchen pump drew on the cistern. In some cases there was yet another well dug near the house that was used as a refrigerator for milk and cream, which were lowered into the well in a bucket.

The windmill, perhaps the most well-recognized structure on the whole farm, stood over the well and pumped on through night and day thanks to the prairie winds (Plates 42, 62). Farmers who had no windmill or ponds or streams on their land were keenly aware of how much water horses and cows needed (about six gallons per head per day) when they had to pump it by hand. The windmill was an efficient machine that required little maintenance except that someone was supposed to climb the tower and grease the gears once a week. That task was sometimes neglected, which caused the common farmyard noise of metal against metal, groaning and shrieking in the wind.

EARLIEST HOUSES

The first houses of the settlers were log cabins built by those who had access to wooded valleys and dugouts and sod houses for those far out on the prairie. Those with a little extra money bought the least expensive lumber and put up a simple shack. Some combined several materials, using sod for walls, logs for roof beams, and boards for the roof itself. All of them were small, typically about nine by thirteen feet, and not very well lit, so some household chores were done outside when weather permitted.

When wood and money were scarce, the settlers cut the prairie sod into blocks and built a dependable house. The sod house, like the igloo, was a direct adaptation to the immediate environment. A well-built soddy was warm in winter and cool in summer because sod was a good insulator. Sod houses were permeable, allowing them to breathe, and also susceptible to mice and insects. A driving rain might damage them but they could be repaired again without much trouble. Settlers typically lived in their primitive homes for up to eight years before they earned enough money to build a permanent house and turn the sod house into a stable for the oxen or horses.

ORIGINS OF THE L-HOUSE

Simple log cabins were built from the seventeenth century in New England to Minnesota in the nineteenth century. Log construction techniques evolved in northern Europe where there were pine, spruce, and other conifers that produced long straight logs that could be used without being split or sawn into planks. If need be a log cabin could be built with no tools except an ax.

Colonial Americans built log houses with one common room where all activities revolved around the hearth. Successful farmers expanded their homes by adding on a new room at right angles to the original house. The new room usually became the kitchen, sometimes called the kitchen L. Bedrooms were built upstairs above the old common room which became the general living room.

This additive process produced designs in which each room had a shape of its own and the final make-up of the house was determined by the way the separate volumes fit together.

THE L-HOUSE ON THE PRAIRIE

The great majority of the houses of western Minnesota were cheap, plain, awkward, and unlovely. Harmony and unity emerged from the mundane clutter, however, in the form of the classic L-house, which became representative of much of the farming way of life in the Midwest. When the prairie families earned enough money to move out of their cabins and sod houses, they often built modest rectangular-shaped, one and a half story houses with simple gable roofs. These structures became L-houses when the families earned enough to add on the kitchen L and porch of a complete L-house.

The easiest way to expand was to extend the original house sideways by laying more joists parallel to the original ones. Since the joist length was limited to about sixteen feet, one ended up with a house sixteen feet wide and whatever length one wanted, but a long narrow house was not very desirable. Those houses were hard to heat evenly, requiring a stove at each end. The next least complicated means of expansion was the L-house approach, which added a second sixteen-foot-wide section onto the side of the original house at right angles so the new floor plan resembled an L where the foot of the L was the living room and the stem of the L was the kitchen. Many L-houses were designed so the living room L segment extended beyond the walls of the kitchen segment, which made the plan resemble an asymmetrical T rather than an L (Plates 24–25, 46). The kitchen was approximately sixteen feet square (Plates 45, 64). The living room, dining room (when present), and upstairs bedrooms were also about sixteen feet square. That sixteen-foot square

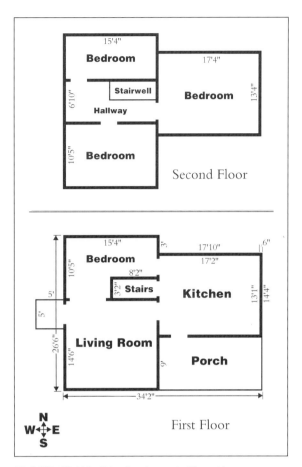

FLOOR PLAN of the farmhouse in Plate 44.

emerges as a sort of module upon measuring the rooms, but it often was not apparent when viewing the house from a distance. The living room L segment as a whole was larger than the kitchen L segment, because it contained a back bedroom about eight by sixteen feet which made the overall dimension about sixteen by twenty-four feet. With the kitchen addition, the house dimensions became thirty-two by twenty-four feet,

The L-house configuration provided good-sized rooms in a fairly compact shape that was easy and economical to build. Many other configurations were possible, but they generally required more complex roofs that were more difficult to build. Further expansion of the L-house was done

by adding on porches, lean-tos, and wings beyond the perimeter of the basic foundation (Plates 13, 59, 61). When yet more space was needed, another section might be added onto the side of the living room, opposite from the kitchen wing, making the new house into a cross form.

THE IDEAL L-HOUSE

The L-house had a long evolution that produced individual houses of almost unlimited variation but, like a species, all the L-houses shared a body of structural design elements—a morphology generated by exercising a given function in a given environment. Every dimension was in flux relative to every other dimension, yet there was a guiding form. The thousands of individual designs clustered around a general ideal that was not necessarily ever built. Perfect examples may well exist somewhere, perhaps in many places, but not in western Minnesota. There the relation between the real and the ideal resembles that advanced by Plato who believed that perfect forms exist only supernaturally, to be striven for but never attained. Farmers, however, did not build in a quest for a philosophical ideal. They drew upon an existing conceptual ideal and adapted it to their specific circumstances.

The farm couple made the decisions that determined the design of the farmhouse. They worked to a greater or lesser degree in consultation with a local house carpenter, and they often selected a local house that they admired to serve as a model or a starting point. They then adapted that design to suit their own particular situation by referring to certain aspects of several other houses that they wished to incorporate into their house. They might like one house for its general size, another for the placement of the kitchen windows, and a third for its number of bedrooms. The new design was generalized or specialized in accordance with their personal experience. The new house would retain most of the design elements of the old houses, but there would be a new emphasis upon those aspects that seemed most important to the success of the family. The general ideal was transmitted through thousands of different houses without being lost.

Unending variations employ most, but not all, of the elements, and the missing or additional or altered elements are different from one house to the next. The size and shape of the house as a whole varies constantly as does the number of rooms and the specific dimensions of each room. The spacing of the windows seems to be different in every house (Plates 25, 28, 34). The height of the springing of the roof, the angle of the roof, and the number of gables and dormers follows no precise rule (Plates 28, 44). Staircases to the bedrooms are extraordinarily individualistic structures that start at different places, rise at a variety of angles (all steep), and turn varying degrees in an effort to minimize wasted space and avoid cutting irregular shapes out of the rooms (Plate 21). Ceiling heights vary not only from one house to the next, but also from one room to the next in the same house. Some houses have a different ceiling height for every room.

There were essentially only four distinct spaces in the prairie L-house—porches, kitchens, bedrooms, and living rooms—and those discrete spaces were sharply defined and not allowed to flow into each other. Most L-houses contained no foyers, alcoves, pantries, or storerooms and few hallways or closets. Rooms were separated with flat walls and simple doors (Plate 45).

PORCHES

The porch was the transition zone between the yard and the house, a staging platform halfway between the comfort and security of the inside and the rigors and demands of the outside. The porch launched and disseminated the family members in the morning, and it gathered them in again

DESIGN ELEMENTS OF THE IDEAL L-HOUSE

1. Standard wood frame construction employing pine 2" x 4"s, 2" x 8"s, and 1" x 10"s, was used throughout (Plate 21).

2. The main floor plan outline was approximately the shape of a broad L or T whose outside dimensions were about 24' by 32' (Plates 24, 33, 39, 49).

3. The main floor plan contained a rectangular or square kitchen about 16' x 16' with an east-west axis joined at right angles to another larger rectangle about 16' x 24' that contained a 16' x 16' living room on the south end, and a back bedroom about 8' x 16' on the north end (Plates 21, 45).

4. An open porch about 5' x 16' with Gothic posts supporting its roof was fit in the angle of the L so the porch overlooked the barnyard and faced the morning light (Plates 24, 36).

5. The outside kitchen and living room doors both opened onto the kitchen porch (Plates 27, 56).

6. There was sometimes a formal front door to the living room and an open front porch on the center of the west end of the house. When a formal front door was present there was usually no living room door opening onto the kitchen porch (Plate 37).

7. The elevation was $1^1/2$ stories high with 4 or 8 pane windows that measured about 28" x 60" evenly spaced on the walls, individually or in pairs, on the vertical center line of the south wall of the living room L (Plates 34, 44).

8. The second floor contained two or three bedrooms whose shapes conformed to the rooms below them. The bedroom above the living room, with the most windows and the most headroom, was usually the master bedroom (Plate 35).

9. Downstairs ceilings were about 9'. The kitchen ceiling was sometimes 1' lower than the living room ceiling. Bedroom ceilings upstairs sloped down at the outside, leaving only about an 8' wide area centered under the roof ridge at full height (Plate 35).

10. The house was sheltered by a pine-shingled gable-ended roof of four basic planes at about 45° to the horizontal with 12" inch over-hangs (Plates 25, 30).

11. There was often an additional gable or gable-ended dormer window fit into the south roof over the kitchen, and over the living room above the front porch, to provide additional windows into the upstairs bedrooms (Plates 28, 44).

12. A two or three window bay was sometimes built out from the south wall of the living room (Plates 44, 52).

13. All outside walls were covered with 4" or 5" pine siding (Plates 20, 37).

14. Exterior decoration was generally restricted to the porch posts, railings, brackets, the gable ends, and the bay window when present (Plates 36, 44).

15. Exteriors were usually painted all white, all one color, or two colors with the darker color applied to door and window frames and selected portions of the decorations.

16. Inside there were three doorways through the wall between the kitchen L and the living room L, one to the living room, one to the second floor bedrooms, and one to the back bedroom on the first floor (Plate 45).

17. There were two square chimneys of brick built on shelves about 6' above the floor. One rose from the kitchen stove up the center of the east wall through the roof ridge, and the other rose from the center of the back wall of the living room L.

18. A grate about 1' square was fit into the ceiling of the living room above the stove, and less commonly above the kitchen stove, to allow warm air to rise into the otherwise unheated upstairs bedrooms.

19. Interior walls and ceilings were covered with lath and plaster and then painted or wallpapered (Plates 21, 57).

20. Floors were of 4" or 5" pine and painted, rarely varnished (Plates 35, 64).

21. There was a small root cellar, about 8' x 12', with a dirt floor under the center of the house, reached through a horizontal door outside and down a wood staircase. (Plate 50).

22. Foundations were of granite fieldstone, about 2' wide, and they were dug down only far enough to get below the frostline—about 3' or 4'.

at the end of the day. Its floor kept people off the ground, and its roof shed the rain, but it allowed most of the wind and light to pass through. On a fine morning the porch invited the family to survey the farm laid out before it and to contemplate the promise of the land while deciding how to proceed with the day's work. It is still satisfying to stand on these porches and look out upon the buildings and through them to the patterned fields beyond. There is a sense of rest, and yet there is an invitation to come and join the music of the fields that the farmer has orchestrated. The porch also gathered in all those who would deal with the workers in the kitchen.

The porch was often designed to fill the area between the two legs of the house, so the perimeter of the house with the porch included formed a rectangle (Plates 29, 30). The width of the porch was usually between five and eight feet, and the length was the same as the length of the kitchen L, which was usually about sixteen feet but might range from ten feet up to thirty feet. If the living room L segment extended farther than five feet beyond the kitchen L segment, the porch might turn and run along the living room wall, making the porch a small L shape nestled in the large L shape of the house (Plate 53). The porch had its own shingled roof extending out from the wall of the house (Plates 24, 37, 54). Usually the pitch of the porch roof was around twenty-five degrees while the house roof was about forty-five degrees. The porch roof was supported by two free-standing posts and two half posts engaged in the walls (Plate 27). The porch floor was built at the same level as the floor of the house, which ranged from a few inches to a foot and a half above the ground. Typically one step was all it took to be in the yard and off to work (Plate 27). Some porches had railings around the perimeter while others had none (Plate 37).

Both the kitchen and the living room had outside doors that opened onto the porch, often with-

in a few feet of each other (Plate 56). Visitors to the living room, the most formal room in the house, did not have to walk through the kitchen, and the family did not have to tramp through the living room to get to the kitchen or to the bedrooms, whose stairway access was in the kitchen (Plate 45).

The porch received the greatest amount of conscious attention to decoration and design aesthetics. It had the finest details of any part of the house and the most sophisticated contrasts between solid volumes and open spaces, between the incised florid line and the broad plane, and between the delicate curve and the power of right and acute angles.

Each porch was decidedly individual even though its posts, brackets, and railings were mass produced in factories because each porch used different combinations of the numerous designs available. The individuality of each porch, set off against the uniform pattern of the siding and shingles, reflected the balance achieved in the nineteenth century between the uniformity of industrial mass production and the independence of each individual, each family, and each farm.

Many L-houses later had their open porches enclosed and covered with the same siding as that used on the rest of the house. Others were turned into screened porches (Plates 54, 59). In both cases the original Gothic posts remained behind the siding or the screens.

The enclosed porch provided a convenient place out of the weather to leave muddy boots, wet coats, and buckets and tools used near the house but not very welcome in the house. The enclosing of the porch made the L-house less attractive because it covered over the only free-standing structural and decorative members (posts, railings, and brackets) on the house that complemented the boxlike structure of the main body of the house. The classic L-house had a pleasing balance between the containing volumes of the body

of the house and the presenting framework of the porches. The structure of the open porch stood confidently in the light and wind and defined a region of space at the entrance to the house that invited transition from the outdoors to the indoors. The enclosed porch looked like an impenetrable box that was defending its contents from a hostile outside world (Plates 23, 43).

KITCHENS

The kitchen was the most important room in the house. It was the one place on the farm that sustained continuous activity all day long from before dawn to bedtime. The kitchen was the base of operations for that entire work day.

The kitchen was usually about sixteen feet square, perhaps 10 percent smaller than the living room on average. In small houses the kitchen tended to be smaller than the living room, and in large houses the kitchen was about equal to the living room (Plates 14, 15). The large houses often had a dining room and a back kitchen in addition to the main kitchen, which allowed the farmwife to spread out her activities. Messy operations like cleaning chickens and doing the laundry took place in the back kitchen where the sink and pump were situated. General cooking and homemaking were conducted in the main kitchen where the stove was, and informal meals were served there. The dining room was reserved for formal meals. In good weather the farmwife might also take some operations like churning butter and peeling potatoes out onto the kitchen porch.

Since the farmwife did most of her work in or near the house, she relied on the windows both to illuminate her work and to oversee outdoor events from within the kitchen. In practice, kitchen interiors were generally well lit, but rarely gracefully or subtly. A sufficient amount of sunlight entered, but little thought was given to controlling the way the light would change through the course of the day to avoid dark corners or to provide easy viewpoints from which to keep track of the weather or to scan the yard. The kitchen was usually not as brightly or evenly lit as the living room, often because it had fewer windows and even those might be under the porch roof, which blocked some of the direct sunlight. In the summer the kitchen door could be left open to allow more light and fresh air to enter through the screen door (Plate 64).

The kitchen had its own chimney for the cookstove, but the room was otherwise plain with no special structures or appliances built into it (Plates 31, 64). Many kitchens had no permanent sink or any sort of plumbing to carry water in or out. The only water that came into the house was carried in, and the sink was wherever one put the pan down—usually on the kitchen table—allowing the farmwife to work in the center of the room. Sooner or later kitchens were fitted with sinks of simple, highly standardized design. They were about six inches deep with outside dimensions of about eighteen by thirty inches. Sinks were hung on the wall with shelf brackets or set in a small stand (Plate 31). There were no hot and cold water faucets at the sink because there was still no plumbing and no hot water heater. The sink was usually placed alone in a corner with no expansive drain boards and counter surfaces surrounding it. When a kitchen pump was installed, it was usually attached to the same simple cabinet or bench that supported the sink. Typically the indoor pump drew water from the cistern that was filled with rain water, which was well suited to washing but less desirable for drinking. Often the sink simply drained into a bucket placed underneath it.

Cooking and washing in the absence indoor plumbing required persistent and determined effort, especially washing in winter when the pump in the yard might be frozen so hot water had to be poured into it, provided one had saved some water for that purpose, to get it thawed and drawing. Standing out in the cold and snow,

SQUAT COOKSTOVES were common in many farmhouse kitchens. *Detail from photo opposite half title page.*

splashing water on your hands and feet in the biting wind, and marching back and forth across the snowy yard carrying pails of water was trying work. Then the water had to be heated on the stove and poured into the washtub. The clothes were rubbed, scrubbed, and wrung out by hand. In winter the wash froze on the line and would take a long time to dry if it was not wrung out well. American manufacturers recognized the difficulty, and, after stoves, wringers were the earliest, widely advertised, mass-produced machines for the home. Once the laundry was finished, all the dirty water had to be lugged out and thrown behind the house where it would not cause trouble. The floor inevitably got wet with all the transferring and splashing, so there was mopping to be done. Some back kitchens had back doors so water could be carried out that way rather than across the front kitchen and the porch. On Saturday night the whole fetching, carrying, and heating operation would be done again for the family's baths.

The prairie farmhouse had both a living room stove and a kitchen stove. On a cold winter night both stoves would be filled with fuel to burn all night. By morning only a few embers remained, and the kitchen stove, which had a smaller capacity, might go out completely. Then, according to one farmer, one had to be careful when using the forks at breakfast because they would stick to one's lip, frozen on, if one didn't warm them first. The classic wood stove provided lively heat and a sense of security and control over one's environment. A full kindling box behind the stove and a tall, dry woodpile in the yard inspired a sense of well being.

None of these farmhouses had fireplaces. Fireplaces required large amounts of wood fuel to keep the house comfortable. At best the fireplace fire put about 5 percent of the heat energy of the wood into the room while the iron stove produced about 25 percent. Eastern farmers had almost unlimited firewood available in the hardwood forests, but the prairie farmer had access to only limited supplies that usually had to be transported many miles. The economics of the situation completely eliminated fireplaces in favor of the iron stove.

A typical stove consisted of about fifty separate pieces, not counting bolts and pipes. About thirty of those parts were castings that could be produced only at a large foundry and not by a local blacksmith.

Brick chimneys were built on shelves about six feet above the foundation, which minimized the number of bricks needed by providing no more chimney than was absolutely necessary. That was another economy measure that seems a little misguided, but one does not find collapsed chimney shelves.

LIVING ROOMS

The living room was usually the largest room in the house. It had more windows than any other room in the house. If the house had a bay window, it was in the living room (Plates 44, 56, 57). Sometimes it had a formal front door and front porch facing a small front yard so little used that it often had no walkway through the grass. The front door and the front porch were among the few structures on the farm that were formal or symbolic rather than functional and practical. The least practical room was the parlor, but true parlors were not often found in these farmhouses, except when the house was unusually large. In small and medium-sized houses the living room was the most formal room—one where family activities other than daily physical work and chores could be conducted. Photographs of relatives hung on the walls, and the family's various mementos and small treasures were kept in a cabinet or on decorative shelves. Many living rooms contained pianos and other musical instruments, which the families played frequently. Books, writing materials, and stereoscope pictures were also kept there.

The living room was to some degree an outpost of civilization or sanctuary. The boundary between the refinements of the living room and the rudeness of the barnyard was abrupt because common farmhouses were like boxes set down upon the land without landscaping transitions like walkways, shrubbery, climbing vines, or flowers. That sharp division is quite apparent when one looks out a living room window. The ground outdoors is not far below floor level, and except for the glass in the window, it is only one step to the prairie grass.

The back one-third of a living room L was sometimes made into a bedroom that was convenient for a grandparent or other aged relative (Plate 45). Occasionally this back room had double doors to the living room, indicating that it might be used as an extension of the living room or as a dining room, especially when it had another door to the kitchen.

BEDROOMS

The bedrooms upstairs had the same floor plan as the rooms on the first floor. The master bedroom was usually over the living room, so it had two windows to the south when the house was ideally situated (Plate 35). The second bedroom was typically over the kitchen, and its principal window was under the gable on the east end of the house. When the kitchen L half of the house was large, the bedroom over the kitchen might have two windows to the east and perhaps one more window in a dormer on the south roof above the kitchen porch. In more elaborate houses that dormer had a door that opened onto a balcony on the roof of the kitchen porch. That arrangement allowed the early morning light to come in the east windows and the full morning light to enter through the balcony doorway.

Hallways were usually minimal and in many cases it was necessary to walk through one bedroom to get to another. Upstairs bedroom ceilings were flat for a width of about eight feet over the center of the room under the roof ridge. Toward the sides of the room, the ceiling sloped down along the underside of the roof to a height of about four or five feet at the outside walls (Plate 35). Quite often the master bedroom was divided into two small bedrooms, each with only a four-foot-wide portion of the ceiling at full height. Then furniture arrangements became limited for fear of blocking the window or the door or hitting one's head on the sloping part of the ceiling. There was little attic space for storage or room for closets.

No insulation was used in the bedroom ceilings or anywhere else in the house. The bedrooms were usually unheated except by warm air rising through a small grate in the living room ceiling or up the stairway from the kitchen when the door at the bottom of the stairs was left open. In some cases, however, the chimney had a stove pipe inlet, indicating that a stove was used in the bedroom. Generally the bedrooms were not personalized for their occupants. Children might play upstairs or do their schoolwork there, but usually the impression is that these people did not spend much time in bed and almost none in the bedrooms otherwise.

SIMPLE HYGIENE

Hygiene and sanitation were practiced in a simple and matter-of-fact way on the farm, and while cleanliness and order were valued highly, it was achieved without a profusion of cosmetic products. Luxurious or self-indulgent grooming was hard to accomplish in a farmhouse with no bathroom and few mirrors. Small wash basins and pitchers of water in the kitchen were used for hand and face washing, and bathing was done in a tub in the middle of the kitchen floor. Such bathing was not conducive to privacy, especially in view of the regular traffic that went through the kitchen door, which might easily include an unexpected neighbor. Blankets or sheets could be hung up around the tub to provide some privacy, and the farmwife often took her bath later in the evening after everyone else.

The absence of a toilet inside the house meant that farm families had to have disciplined digestive systems that did not require trips to the outhouse in the middle of a stormy night. Chamber pots might be provided in the bedrooms, but their use was awkward and to be avoided except as a last resort. Generally the use of the outdoor toilet was simply accepted as a fact of life that was no more distressing than a hundred other aspects of farm life that had some element of unpleasantness or inconvenience to them. During the day when they were working outside anyway, the men found the outhouse to be perfectly satisfactory and even convenient to the extent that they continued to use it even after the installation of indoor toilets. The women found much to admire in indoor plumbing, but their comfort does not appear always to have been considered critical; some classic farmhouses never did have an indoor toilet, even though they were occupied into the 1970s.

Practically every farm employed a different combination of technologies operating at varying levels of modernity. Some farmers got modern plumbing and lighting soon after it became available, while others might not put in a modern system until fifty or sixty years later, especially with regard to indoor toilets, hot and cold running water, and septic tanks and drainfields to manage sewage. On the other hand, farmers with wet fields were quick to dig drainage ditches and install drain tile under those fields to dry them out. Even quite humble farms acquired telephones and radios shortly after they came into use, because they provided an immediate sense of communion with the greater society beyond the borders of the farm and greatly diminished the loneliness and monotony that sometimes settled upon the farm.

FOUNDATIONS

The foundations that supported the house were made of granite and gneiss boulders that were left by the glaciers and collected out of the fields by the farmers. Size varied from a maximum of about twenty inches to a minimum of about four inches in diameter. The stones were often graduated in size so large stones appear at the bottom and small stones near the top (Plate 50). They were igneous and metamorphic rocks that did not break into planar shapes as did sedimentary rocks like limestone. The stones appear to have been cemented together with a well-prepared portland type of cement that did not crumble excessively. Generally very little was

used between the stones, which left them somewhat precariously balanced among small disconnected hunks of cement rather than bound together in a continuous matrix. The foundations of practically all the nineteenth-century farmhouses have broken apart due to skimpy use of cement (Plates 23, 44, 60). Usually the stones were used just as they were found in the field, but sometimes broken rock was arranged in such a way that all outward faces were flat, which produced a more square and formal looking foundation. Some foundations contain rocks that show fresh surfaces never ground by glacial action, and they bear occasional drill marks, suggesting that they were collected from the waste rock of quarry operations in the Minnesota River Valley.

The width of the foundation walls under medium and large houses was about twenty-four to thirty inches and under small houses about eighteen inches. The foundations lay under both the perimeter of the house and the interior load-bearing walls. The perimeter foundation was carried down only deep enough to clear the frost line at about three or four feet and not down the seven or eight feet that would have been required to build the walls for full basements. A full basement would have necessitated major excavation and much more rock and cement. Moreover the farm families did not require extensive underground storage space. Instead there was typically only one rather small room dug out under the middle of the house to serve as a root cellar (Plate 50). Those cellars had dirt floors and wooden shelves to store home-canned goods and not much else since these homes had no furnaces, water heaters, laundry tubs, plumbing, or electric wires that needed to be put in a basement. Access to the cellar was through an outside entrance with a stairway covered by a sloping door near ground level (Plates 12, 13, 48). In large houses there was usually also a wooden staircase leading down to the cellar

from the kitchen. In small houses the cellar was about eight by sixteen feet and in large houses it ranged up to sixteen by twenty-four feet.

Most foundations were built up to about twelve inches above ground level and left visible, with no transition between the foundation stones and the horizontal pattern of the exterior wood siding. Occasionally a wider piece of siding was placed at the bottom of the wall, which created a visual transition between the siding and the foundation (Plates 15, 26). Sometimes the top of the foundation was only a few inches above the ground, which meant that the bottoms of the floor joists were also near the ground level. Usually the joist ends were laid directly upon the top of the foundation without benefit of the two-by-six-inch sill that was placed between the joists and the foundation in the standard frame construction of city dwellings of that time (Plate 50). That seems like an unwise shortcut, especially in view of the irregular sized stones used in the foundations, but there is usually no evidence of instability resulting from it. These economies in site preparation and transition structures between house and land do, however, contribute

A FOUNDATION made of rock and held together with cement supported the farmhouses.

to the impression that the prairie farmhouse was simply set on the ground (Plates 47, 53).

CONSTRUCTION

The housebuilders on the prairie built with small dimension, sawmill-generated lumber joined together with factory-produced wire nails. They employed the balloon-frame technique, which was devoid of complex joints that required difficult cutting, fitting, or boring, and no special skills were required to raise a light, strong building quickly. That method was a natural outcome of the technology, resources, and economy in effect at the time of the boom in wheat, lumber, and railroading. Its use was indigenous to the Midwest.

The underlying determinant of room dimensions was the maximum span that could be efficiently crossed by two-by-eight-inch floor joists. Most builders used sixteen-foot planks that resulted in a twelve-foot free span between the two-foot-wide foundation walls, and a fifteen-foot free span between the walls supporting the second floor because the walls were about six inches thick and stood with their outer edges flush with the outside of the foundation. That approach produced maximum room width with a minimum amount of material and floors that were reasonably strong and rigid. Beyond that the floor might be springy and the plaster would crack off the ceiling. Planks of eighteen and twenty feet were also used with some frequency, but long, unsupported planks were not strong or practical. Long logs were harder to get out of the woods, unwieldy to float to the mills, and awkward to saw, stack, and transport. Planks up to at least twenty-eight feet could be obtained, but they cost more per foot than the shorter lengths. Greater distances could be spanned if deeper planks (two-by-ten-inch or two-by-twelve-inch) were used or if the joists were placed closer together, but that was rarely done because of the cost. While the

rooms in an average farmhouse were a little larger than those of a comparable house in town, the farm family did not need huge rooms. Big families and threshing crews could fit into medium-sized kitchens, living rooms, or dining rooms or be accommodated in shifts. Large social gatherings were held outdoors with the possible option of retreat to the barn in the event of rain.

The standard spacing between floor joists, wall studs, and roof rafters was sixteen inches, center to center (Plates 21, 30, 50). Floor joists were sometimes spaced a little wider to about twenty inches, especially where the joists passed just above the ground and could be partially supported by stones placed on the ground at several points along their length. Sometimes two-by-six-inch boards were used under floors of short span and almost always under the porch floor.

FLOORS

Floor joists were overlaid by one-by-ten-inch subflooring boards at right angles across the joists followed by the flooring laid at right angles over the subflooring. Flooring was usually five-inch-wide tongue-and-groove pine, almost clear except for a few solid knots, but it came in many different widths and grades.

The lumbermen of the Mississippi Valley preferred to avoid proliferating sizes and grades compared to the lumbermen of Chicago. The latter sold to a greater variety of builders than did the river men and could make more money by creating many subdivisions, which prompted the river men to assert that some Chicago yards had as many grades as they did boards. Even the river men produced a bountiful array of sizes, lengths, widths, and grades in all their forms, including boards, planks, pickets, shingles, and siding.

In the best houses, the floors were four-inch clear pine with no knots whatsoever and with

long runs of close, straight grain. Those floors were varnished so the grain was visible while the ordinary floor was painted a flat color—typically light gray. A few large houses had maple floors. Oak played no part in these farmhouses. Oak, maple, fir, and cedar were cut in Minnesota forests along with red and white pine, but only in small quantities, and it rarely appeared in farmhouse construction.

The porch floor was of one-by-four-inch, tongue-and-groove pine running crosswise out from the house and resting on two-by-six inch joists running the length of the porch (Plates 18, 37, 46). Subflooring was not used, and porch foundations usually were separate from those of the house and of smaller size, which almost always resulted in uneven settling between the house and the porch foundations so the porch tilted away from the house (Plate 38). A flat, six-inch molding ran around the base of the porch. The bottom of the molding aligned with the bottom of the siding on the house. If the porch floor was more than a foot above the yard, crisscrossed lath might be placed below the base molding, and a simple wooden step provided a link between the porch floor and the ground.

WALLS

The house walls were six inches thick with the outside one and one-half inch of the siding and outside wall board extending beyond the ends of the joists and the outside foundation wall so water dripping off the siding would fall just clear of the foundation. The stud within the wall was a little under four inches wide and the lath and plaster attached to it were about three-fourths inch thick, making the total thickness of the wall about six inches (Plate 21).

Outside walls were covered with one by ten inch sheathing nailed to the studs, followed by four-inch horizontal lap siding that abutted four-inch flat molding running vertically at the corners of the house. Siding, like flooring, came in various sizes, but four-inch, four and one-half-inch, and five-inch were the most commonly used. Gable ends were often patterned with special siding. Sometimes a layer of building paper was placed between the sheathing and the siding.

ROOFS

Roofs were built of two-by-four-inch rafters covered by one-by-ten-inch boards similar to the way walls were built, except that the distance between the two-by-fours was often a little greater than the sixteen-inch, center-to-center standard measure—perhaps twenty to twenty-four inches. (Plates 30, 58). The shingles were sawed, not split, from clear pine. They were sixteen inches long and of varying widths ranging between three and twelve inches. They tapered from about five-sixteenths inch at the front edge to about one-sixteenth inch at the back edge. Special sizes and shapes were used to decorate the gables and on the little roofs over bay windows (Plates 19, 44). Those shingles might be shorter and thinner, about twelve inches long and tapering from three-sixteenths to one-sixteenth inch, and they were available in a variety of styles, including pointed, rounded, and wavy.

Shingles were nailed in place with standard one and one-fourth-inch wire nails and overlapped to leave about a five-inch face exposed to the weather. That system created a roof of three layers with a thickness of about three-fourth-inch. The joints between the sides of two shingles were always staggered to be over an unbroken shingle face below them so no water could fall straight through a series of cracks vertically aligned through all three layers. Most of the water ran down the outer faces without getting between the cracks because the spaces were slim, except for a few minutes at the beginning of a

rainfall before the shingles absorbed water and swelled to close the edge joints. A mature attic roof or barn roof might show hundreds of rays of light beaming through when it was dry, but a few minutes after it began to rain, all those little cracks closed up as the pine expanded (Plate 11). The shingles might be soaked in water before they were nailed in place so they would expand to the same size that they would be during a rainfall, although usually the roofer simply allowed about an eighth of an inch by eye. If no allowance was made for the expansion, the roof would ripple and buckle when the shingles expanded. The shingles were used in their natural state with no paint or oil applied to them, nor was tar paper laid on the roof boards before the shingles went on. These roofs breathed easily, and the spaces under them required no ventilators to remove excess heat or moisture, except in barns. In fact the roofs would naturally refrigerate a little when the sun and wind evaporated the water absorbed in a rainfall or during the night.

The roofs and foundations of these houses were their most vulnerable parts because they were most often wet or moist. When the house finally failed, it was almost always because the roof began to leak or because the foundation came apart and stones fell in. Once water penetrated a neglected roof, it seeped into boards, ran down rafters and studs, and soaked into ceilings and walls, causing the plaster to loosen and fall (Plate 58). In long-abandoned houses, the first floor will be rotted out under the place where the second floor rotted out under the ceiling that fell through under the hole in the roof, leaving a column of space and light rising from the ground to the sky.

These roofs were trustworthy defenders of the rest of the structure because they never rested. They were always moving and breathing and heating and cooling because they were always

absorbing and evaporating in the changing weather. Some appear to have served for upward of a hundred years, requiring only minor maintenance. The weather faces of the shingles bear witness to the relentless attention of the sun, rain, wind, frost, lichens, and moss. Pine is not of itself a permanent material, like slate or tile, and some shingles still in place today have eroded down to less than half their original thickness, yet they are still shedding rain and resisting the weather.

Much of the water shed by the roof was allowed to drip straight to the ground, but usually several sides of the roof were fitted with gutters that ran into drainpipes that emptied into the concrete cistern, which was normally located under the corner of the kitchen with the pump (Plates 46, 47). That water was stored to be used for all types of washing because it was soft (free of mineral salts) and mixed easily with soap. The cisterns were about five or six feet in diameter and eight feet deep. They were shaped like big canning jars, and they were sunk into the ground deep enough to keep the water from freezing in winter. The top of the cistern had sloping shoulders and a neck about two feet high covered by a wooden lid about two feet in diameter.

INTERIORS

Interiors were essentially simple boxes with doorways between them. Walls and ceilings were usually finished with lath and plaster even in the smallest and cheapest houses. The only functional reason to plaster the walls was to minimize drafts that would draw the heat out of the house in winter. Plaster was no guarantee against heat loss, however, because it was not a good insulator itself, and cold air could still leak in around ill-fitting doors, windows, and floor moldings. Some rooms were finished with horizontal boards and then covered with wallpaper. That method was cheaper and less desirable than plaster, and it was usually employed in the least formal rooms or rooms finished subsequent to the original plaster work.

Finishing walls and ceilings with lath and plaster was an expensive and time-consuming practice that required special skill. The wages of a plasterer were higher than those of any other kind of worker involved in house building. To plaster a wall or ceiling, thousands of strips of rough-sawed lath (five-sixteenths by one and three-eighths inches by four feet) had to be nailed in place about three-eighths inch apart across all the studs and rafters (Plates 21, 31, 32). Then wet plaster was applied with a trowel and pressed firmly against the lath so the plaster squeezed through the cracks left between the lath strips and sagged down behind the lath. The plaster formed long hooks when it hardened that locked the plaster on the wall. Even more skill was required to plaster ceilings. The plaster had to be mixed thin enough to squeeze through the lath but thick enough not to sag and fall off the ceiling. Classic plaster was applied in two or more layers. The base layer was about one-fourth to one-half inch thick, and it had sand and animal hair mixed into it, while the finishing layer was pure plaster applied about one-eighth inch thick. The animal hair formed a binding matrix that resisted cracking and held the plaster in place when it did crack. Pieces of fallen plaster in the abandoned houses often broke cleanly, however, showing few binding strands, which may have been another economy measure. Sometimes the houses had a modernized sort of lath made of boards with grooves cut in them for the plaster to adhere to instead of having spaces between them for the plaster to hook into. That sort of lath did not hold the plaster as securely, and it fell away in sheets, while plaster falls away from classic lath in small hunks and

plates typically where it was not squeezed far enough through the spaces to form the hooks.

Walls were painted off-white or light hues of beige or blue. The colors usually appear to have been composed of a little hue and a lot of white so the rooms were generally light and radiant. On rare occasions rooms were decorated with stenciled floral patterns around the borders of the walls. Those patterns also were generally quite subtle. They were composed of closely related hues or complementary hues of quite similar value. Stenciled walls may have been more common than they now appear to be. There may be quite a bit of it hidden under subsequent layers of paint and wallpaper, but the general practice was not to decorate extensively. Most of the time rooms were decorated conservatively to remain in the background behind the important working objects in the room.

Woodwork was standardized in accordance with the common forms available from the industrial millwork companies and did not receive much emphasis. Baseboard moldings were about eight inches high and formed from

F. L. JOHNSON CO.,

WHOLESALE MANUFACTURERS OF

DOORS, SASH AND MOULDINGS.

WINDOW & DOOR FRAMES,

Newell Posts, Balusters, Stair Railing,

MANTLES, PEW ENDS, CHURCH FINISH,

And all kinds of plain and ornamental Building Material.

GLAZED SASH.

Price Lists, Moulding Book, Estimates, or any other information in our line, furnished on application.

Cor. 3d St. and 3d Ave. S., - - MINNEAPOLIS, MINN.

LOCAL LUMBER YARDS sold farmers the same complex building components that were sought after by city builders. *Mississippi Valley Lumberman and Manufacturer,* Minneapolis, Minn. October 18, 1878.

two or three separate pieces, just as they were in city houses (Plates 35, 57). Doorways and windows were enframed by ribbed moldings about six inches wide, and square corner blocks were fitted into the upper corners (Plates 45, 64). Circles or four-part abstract designs resembling leaves were cut into most of them. About four or five basic designs account for practically all the houses that have corner-block moldings. Some houses have four- or five-inch window and door moldings with no ribs and no corner pieces (Plate 16). Windows were mounted in double tracks, but they were not counterbalanced with ropes, pulleys, and sash weights. Doors were constructed of solid pine of light frame-and-panel design. Front doors were sometimes decorated with sunburst patterns, garlands, or leaf forms (Plates 27, 57). Wainscoting was occasionally used in kitchens or in dining rooms that were originally kitchens (Plates 31, 64).

Practically all the woodwork was pine and was painted or hand-grained to resemble oak. Doors could be purchased with grain already applied, or a grainer could be employed to finish the woodwork once it was in place. Grainers' advertisements may be found with some frequency in local newspapers while house carpenters and contractors are almost never mentioned. The grainers were also the ones who painted the stenciling and hung the wallpaper. Their oak graining can be found under subsequent layers of paint even in some of the smallest houses where the greatest economies were otherwise employed. While the overall coloring of the graining generally resembled oak, many of the grain patterns looked as much like pine as they did oak. Real oak doors could have been produced almost as economically, but they never were. Natural hardwood woodwork did not became common until the period 1893–1919, but in the classic period, 1862–1893, hardwood interiors were usually found only in city houses.

38

A FULLY DEVELOPED CLASSIC L-HOUSE, such as this one photographed in Lac qui Parle County in 1895, would employ almost all of the basic L-house design elements along with some aspect that was atypical. In this case it is the location of the back door and the little back porch. Minnesota Historical Society

HARD EXPERIENCE ON THE LAND rather than philosophical musing on the drawing board produced the layout and design of the L-house. It was an intangible pattern, usually an image, fluctuating in the memory of persons sharing a common experience. It performed the same function culturally as genes perform biologically. That is, it could perpetuate its form as a dematerialized pattern through the nervous system of a host human being and reproduce itself in tangible form in a future material environment. Such forms may be codified into written specifications, plans, and drawings that make them available to those who have not lived through their evolutionary generation as firsthand experience, but those do not appear to be the methods used to transmit the form of the L-house

from one farm to another. The L-houses appear to be a product of the dissemination of general knowledge by example and by the spoken word within an unconscious process of folk evolution that proceeded largely independent from written descriptions and published plans. They are the products of individual decision and judgment in response to immediate local conditions, unlike developer-built row houses, tract houses, apartment buildings, and suburban parks, which are not designed by the persons who live in them.

The lives of western farmers were governed by the availability of economical, industrially produced building materials that obliged the farmers to build farms aesthetically consistent with the real economic forces of their times whether they knew

it or not. The object ought to be to examine the structures that were actually built within their total environment, to determine the economies practiced in the work spaces and living spaces defined by the buildings, and to respect the lives and human values that resulted from the effort. Farmers might have liked to have had a fancy house because that would have demonstrated financial success sufficient to purchase the forms that were favored by the established powers in the East, but the expression of those conforming aesthetic ideals took more money than most families had. Necessity kept their houses plain, and their forms resulted from hard living in the West.

Anyone yearning to find a romantic and idyllic basis for farm life and the evolution of its structures will yearn in vain because such beauty as they possess resulted from practical necessity and not from an imposed aesthetic philosophy. On the other hand, those who admire the power and productivity of the warmhearted farm family will find much to marvel at in the integrity of their way of life and much to affirm one's faith in human nature upon seeing how much could be accomplished under such rudimentary living conditions in such simple structures.

The classic farm was not a permanent ideal whose form could be perpetuated indefinitely, but rather a structural species evolved through adaptation to a specific set of economic conditions. Classic farm life on the prairie developed quickly and produced only one wave of characteristic architecture. Once the hunger of world markets for wheat was satisfied by the exploitation of the virgin land, the motivation to generate an original regional economy diminished and indigenous architecture ceased to be produced. There was nothing built there before the farmers came, and nothing built there since that time really belongs to the region. The realization of the dream consumed the basis for the dream, and the next dream has not yet formed.

THE PLATES

Photographs by William G. Gabler

PLATE 2. IN THE UPPER MINNESOTA RIVER VALLEY near Ortonville, rounded masses of granite and gneiss rise from the valley floor and testify to the great age of the basement rock lying just beneath the youthful soil and to the primal nature of the processes of wind and water that produced the prairie. Here the trees of the valley stand in early spring floodwaters, which are held in the valley by dams designed to maintain the wetlands. These masses of rock were quarried for building stone that sometimes ended up in farmhouse foundations. Big Stone County

PLATE 3. THE BUFFALO more than any other living thing seemed to embody the unquenchable life force of the prairie environment. The species was by no means inviolate, however, and in geological terms it was destroyed instantly, leaving only a tiny remnant when it came in contact with industrial human culture. This female buffalo lives in Blue Mounds State Park. Rock County

PLATE 4. FLAT OR GENTLY UNDULATING TERRAIN is typical of most Minnesota prairie regions, although there are some areas of more steeply rolling hills, like those of the Coteau des Prairies in eastern South Dakota. The hills rise about two hundred feet above the surrounding prairie. They are composed of terminal moraine that was heaped up at the front of the glacier, while the surrounding plain was formed by more evenly deposited ground moraine. Yellow Medicine County

PLATE 5. THE MEANDERING STREAMS of western Minnesota cut into the glacial till to reveal the soil profile. Originally the topsoil was about three to four feet thick. Now the topsoil ranges from a few inches to about two feet thick. The topsoil is quite black, the subsoil dark brown, and the glacial-till parent material yellow brown. Lac qui Parle County

PLATE 6. PRAIRIE FARMERS PLANT ROWS OF TREES on the west and north sides of their farmsteads to control the wind. The outside, or windward, row of the shelterbelt planted in accordance with U.S. Department of Agriculture recommendations is composed of dense low shrubs. They slow down the wind traveling closest to the ground, which causes the wind to drop its snow load in the space between the shrubs and the first row of trees. The resulting snowdrifts persist well into spring, long after the fields are snow free. Young shelterbelts like this one perform with almost scientific predictability. Old shelterbelts usually have no snow catcher row of shrubs, and they cause snow to accumulate among the trees and on their lee-side in the yard around the house. Yellow Medicine County

PLATE 7. WILD SUNFLOWERS take over a field temporarily withdrawn from crop production. Colonies of wildflowers display a multiplicity of individuality, different from the monotonous replications that field crops demonstrate. The wildflowers vary in height, size, and time of bloom, while domestic sunflowers grow with great uniformity and almost mechanical regularity. Lac qui Parle County

PLATE 8.   IN WINTER THE WIND blows loose snow and dust off the fields and into the ditches where it displays complicated wave patterns. Some are streaked and stratified like dune sand, some are rippled like waves on water, and some are scalloped like frosting on a cake. The patterns reveal the presence of untamed natural forces that underlie the human geometry on the surface of the land. Big Stone County

PLATE 9. EARLY GRAIN ELEVATOR BUILDERS employed frame construction methods similar to those used to build farmhouses, but the walls of those elevators tended to bulge, so a stronger method was devised. They stacked up two-by-fours face to face, spiked them together, and interlocked them at the corners to form tall containers with solid wood walls four inches thick. The compartments were about ten feet square on the ground and forty to fifty feet high. The elevator as a whole typically contained twelve vertical compartments. As railroad service was withdrawn from rural regions, and the towns shrank, truckers took over grain shipment from new elevators designed to load their trucks, and the old elevators became subject to demolition. Vayland, South Dakota

PLATE 10. PLANK BARNS, built entirely from industrially produced boards (planks) one or two inches thick, were the most common type of barn in Minnesota in the classic period between 1863 and 1893. They were typically about thirty-six feet wide, thirty feet tall and any length one wanted—usually between forty and fifty feet. Plank barns were expanded by adding lean-tos to shelter animals or make a toolshed. The only access to the hay floor was by a ladder inside or through the big hay door to the outside. The hay was lifted with a rope over a pulley up under the roof overhang. A horse on the ground pulled the rope and lifted the hay to a person standing in the hay doorway who then guided the hay into the barn by pulling it along, suspended from a track that ran the entire length of the roof ridge. Yellow Medicine County

PLATE 11. THE LARGE AMOUNT OF HAY (as much as one hundred tons) needed to carry the animals through the winter required a big building in which to store it. The voluminous hayloft of the gambrel-roofed plank barn, unobstructed by posts or crossbeams, fulfilled that need, and the track that ran along under the roof ridge allowed bundles of loose hay to be rolled in and dropped in place with more efficiency than could be accomplished with hand forks. With the possible exception of an occasional church, these haylofts were the largest interior spaces to be found anywhere on the prairie. Yellow Medicine County

PLATE 12.   FARMERS EXPANDED SIMPLE, HUMBLE HOUSES by adding lean-tos whose roofs extended down and out from the back roof of the house. As those roofs were extended, they got closer to the ground, so the angle of the lean-to roof was necessarily less than that of the main roof. At least two stages of expansion appear to have been done here with a decrease in the pitch of the roof each time. The first stage included a new kitchen door beside the old original door. Then that new door (behind the tree branches) appears to have been abandoned when the porch was built. Lac qui Parle County

PLATE 13. THE ORIGINAL L-HOUSE, formed by the two segments to the left is about as small as one ever sees. The center section is the living room L, and it measures fourteen by twenty feet. The kitchen L, to the far left, measures twelve by fourteen feet. Originally there was only one bedroom, above the living room, and it had so little headroom that one could not stand upright in any part of it. The addition of the twelve-by-twenty foot lean-to gave the house a longer, lower appearance that was more characteristic of ranch houses farther west than it was of prairie houses in Minnesota. This house was finished in standard fashion with lath-and-plaster walls; underneath the peeling paint on the doorframes one finds simulated oak grain. The shed in the background was built from fieldstone, which was usually employed only in foundations. Lac qui Parle County

PLATE 14. THE TYPICAL L-HOUSE was a plain and general structure that was subject to various alterations in the course of its existence. Here all the windows on the end of the living room appear to be offset to the left, and there is a vertical joint line in the siding to the right, which implies that the house was enlarged by about four feet to the right. The house was also extended to the left by building an enclosed porch onto the end of the kitchen L, so the kitchen L looks like a tunnel leading to the inner chamber of the living room. The formal front of the house is largely undeveloped. It has only a plain front door with no porch or even a stoop. Lac qui Parle County

PLATE 15. THIS TYPICAL LITTLE L-HOUSE has a more or less standard living room L at about eighteen by twenty-four feet with a small gable-roofed kitchen L segment. It contains a living room in the front with inside dimensions of twelve feet three inches by seventeen feet two inches. Behind the living room there is a back bedroom of nine feet eight inches by ten feet four inches, space for the staircase, and a pantry of about four by five feet that served the kitchen. The kitchen has outside dimensions of eleven feet eight inches by twelve feet four inches which are about average minimums. Kitchens smaller than that will not accommodate a full size kitchen table. The atypical enclosed porch appears to have been pieced together in a makeshift fashion sometime after the kitchen was built.
Grant County, South Dakota

PLATE 16. ON RARE OCCASIONS one finds a room that still can generate images infused with something of the spirit of the occupants. The energy, enthusiasm, and delight of childhood seem to have left a lasting impression upon this room where the patterns and forms of the out door world enter and assert themselves indoors. It is likely that these two wallpaper patterns do not predate the 1940s, and it may be that no child ever lived in this room (in the house pictured in Plate 15), but the room still seems to contain a memory of the wonder-infused life of children. Renville County

PLATE 17. WITH ITS YARD SPACES STILL INTACT and in original proportion to the driveway and the shelterbelt, this house almost appears to be functioning today, although the trees and shrubs have begun to take over. Yellow Medicine County

PLATE 18. A FARMHOUSE WITH STYLISTIC CONSISTENCY throughout its parts has survived and revealed its Victorian architecture. It has its original pine shingles and four-pane windows, and both the front porch and the bay window seem to be essentially whole and original. The house appears to have been designed in its entirety by someone with a knowledge of professional architecture. A somewhat ornate chimney, eve extensions beneath the dormer roof , lintels over the windows, and the decorative trim on the front porch and bay window all contain Victorian or Gothic revival design elements that had little or no physical function. Yellow Medicine County

PLATE 19. ONLY TWO ESSENTIAL VOLUMES, the rectangular main house and the truncated wedge of the lean-to, make up the whole form of this house (pictured from the front in Plates 17 and 18). The shack-like character of the back of the house is decidedly different from the delicately decorated front portion. The kitchen-stove chimney above the lean-to was pieced together from sections of drain pipe, while the living room chimney above the main house was built of brick, which gives the impression that the lean-to was added at a later, but not necessarily more prosperous, time. Yellow Medicine County

PLATE 20. AS ABANDONED HOUSES DECAY they come apart in approximately the reverse of the order of their construction. The simplicity of the essential shell of the house becomes apparent when the porches, doors, windows, and window frames disappear. The individual personality of the house fades, and the more mechanical aspects of the design and construction are revealed. This house appears to be normally situated with the kitchen porch and living room windows facing the driveway, which is behind the camera. It is atypical insofar as this is the north side of the house. The kitchen porch and living room windows would normally be on the south side of the house, and the driveway would pass in front of them. Yellow Medicine County

PLATE 21. THE OUTSIDE WORLD INVADES AN ABANDONED HOUSE (pictured in Plate 20)
through the doors and windows and, sooner or later, the roof. The plaster is quick to absorb extra moisture,
which separates it from the lath and sends it to the floor. The living room chimney is suspended in the air by
the chimney shelf (top center). The long diagonal two-by-fours carry the weight at the outside edge of the
chimney shelf back to the wall studs. The chimney is fit to the wall so the wall carries the weight and spreads
the load. The kitchen is at the far left, and the back bedroom is behind the chimney. The stairway from the
second floor comes down into a sort of utility room-pantry that opens into the kitchen. Yellow Medicine County

PLATE 22.   L-HOUSES BUILT IN THE EASTERN PORTION of the Minnesota River Valley may be thirty years older than similar shaped houses at the western end of the valley. This house has a front door centered between the first floor windows on the end of the living room L, representing a style found on L-houses built near Minneapolis and St. Paul, but rarely in the western half of the state. Serious flooding in 1993 forced the owner out for several weeks, demonstrating the virtue of building on a hill, but the house has been flooded numerous times without being destroyed, and the present owner has now moved back in. Normally the river follows its bed under the bridge barely visible at the extreme right of the picture. Carver County

PLATE 23. THIS STRUCTURE IS ESSENTIALLY an L-house built within the range of standard proportions, and it has a porch in the usual position, but the house lacks proportionate coordination among
its parts and between itself and the environment. The mystifying placement of the windows gives little
indication of the character of the rooms they serve (the kitchen chimney, to the right, appears to come
down in front of the bedroom window), and the broad blank areas of wall and roof are at a different scale
from that of the compressed design of the enclosed porch. The house is a closed form with little extension
into the environment. The shabby disorder of the house and yard implies that life on a Minnesota farm
could be as crude, careless, and joyless as in any city slum. Lac qui Parle County

PLATE 24. THE SIMPLE SHAPES, uninterrupted planes, and absence of paint on this house give it a
primitive, rural robustness reminiscent of some of its log cabin predecessors, but the materials and methods
of construction are products of the industries of the cities. The vertical rows of nail heads visible on the
living room wall siding trace the position of the studs, which rise unbroken from the sill on the foundation
to the rafters except where they are cut out to accommodate standard, factory-produced window casings.
The south-facing kitchen porch is a near perfect example of classic L-house porch design. Of all the
houses visited this one seemed most to embody the healthy and unpretentious vigor of the pioneer spirit.
The house has now disappeared. Lac qui Parle County

PLATE 25. THE HOUSE IN PLATE 24, seen here from the north, still looks alert and alive with individual
personality, perhaps because the upstairs windows are a little like eyes with curtains for eyelids and the springing
point of the roof is low while the eaves are long so the sheltering hat-like character of the roof is emphasized.
This view of the house appears more detailed and feminine than the front view, partly because the paint stays
on the north side of a house longer, and because of the curtain remnants in the windows, but also because the
porch is larger and more elaborate than the one on the south. The delicate brackets and railings and the multi-
paneled door imply that this side of the house was built later. Like many L-houses, this is actually a T-house
with projections to the left and right of the axis of the original kitchen L. Lac Qui Parle County

PLATE 26.   L-HOUSES BUILT IN TOWN had shapes and styles similar to those built on farms, but the proportions sometimes were a little different. On average, L-houses in town were smaller, more compact, and more vertical. They also tended to have fewer wings, lean-tos, and extra rooms added to the original house. Here the kitchen L is shorter than the width of the living-room L, which resulted in a small kitchen and a short porch. This house is now gone. Redwood County

PLATE 27. THIS PORCH (from the house pictured in Plate 26) has all the classic L–house porch
design elements assembled in an unusually compact configuration. The living room and the kitchen
doors open onto the porch within a few feet of each other. The decoration of the front door includes
an etched glass window. Such windows were often selected from catalogs, as were the railings, posts, and
brackets. The porch railing is still in place, showing how it fit against the squared lower portion of the
post. Redwood County

PLATE 28. THE SITUATION OF THIS HOUSE and the arrangement of its rooms are typical of Minnesota L-houses. The kitchen porch opens to the east and to the south where the barnyard lies, and the formal front of the house faces the road to the north. The house looks rather flat faced when viewed straight on because the roof overhangs are short, the windows are plain, and there is no projecting bay window. The front of the house also appears a little more horizontally extended than the average because the gables are moderately low, with gable angles slightly greater than ninety degrees. Lac Qui Parle County

PLATE 29. A FEW HOUSES REMAIN almost unchanged since the time they were built. This house has no additions and no missing parts, except that modern asphalt shingles have replaced the pine-shingle roof. Well-kept farmhouses originally looked something like this, although old photos document that many farmhouses were continually changing and never looked finished and complete. Most kitchen porches face both the morning light and the barnyard, but this kitchen porch faces south, away from the barnyard and toward the township road. The formal front of the house is undeveloped and overlooks the driveway, which atypically passes the house on the west instead of the east. An additional door was built into the back of the kitchen for direct exit toward the barnyard. Lac Qui Parle County

PLATE 30.   OFTEN THE PORCH is the only part of a basic or simple L-house that saves the house from looking plain and characterless. In this view the porch appears to be built of nothing but a roof and two posts, but those elements are nicely proportioned and balanced so the space they define has a comfortable and inviting look that enhances the hospitality of the house. The weather has dismantled the roof and revealed how many hundreds of small, individual pieces were put together to complete it. The trend in modern house-building is to use one big premanufactured piece (twenty-eight-foot roof trusses, four-by-eight-foot chipboard panels) where in the past, ten to a hundred small pieces would have been hand assembled onto the house. Big Stone County

PLATE 31.   FEW ROOMS REMAIN today that contain the furnishings of the old way of life before the installation of plumbing and electricity. When this kitchen (in the house pictured in Plate 30) was abandoned, the occupant was still cooking on a woodburning stove, although this stove was being fired with corncobs and charcoal rather than wood. Dry corncobs were good fuel, and these stoves were advertised as designed to burn wood, coal, or corncobs equally well. The presence of all these objects is evidence of the variety of regular physical labor that was required to get clean water and sound fuel into the kitchen and waste water, garbage, ashes, and smoke out of the kitchen safely and efficiently. The door behind the stove leads to the back bedroom and also to the stairs to the second floor, the one to the right of the stove leads to the cellar. Big Stone County

PLATE 32. IN SOUTH CENTRAL MINNESOTA the prairie to the west met the hardwood forest to the east and formed park lands where the trees were interspersed with grass. Early farmers built houses of squared logs cut from the local woods in the years before economical pine lumber became available in the 1870s. This house was built in two stages. The first house was built of squared logs perhaps in the 1860s, then it was expanded into an L-house by adding on a living room L section built with standard sawmill lumber. The log house became the kitchen and the logs were covered over inside and outside to make the composite house appear unified. After the house was abandoned, the foundations under the log house came apart, and it fell into its own cellar. Carver County

PLATE 33. THE VIEW ACROSS THE FRONT YARD to the formal front of an L-house may convey the impression that the house is composed of only a single unit when, in fact, it is a compound house as seen from another angle (see Plate 34). Horizontal lines dominate the east end of this house except for a few verticals and diagonals within the design cluster surrounding the front door. Chippewa County

PLATE 34. MANY ASPECTS OF THE CLASSIC L-HOUSE appear in this farmhouse, which was one of the three most nearly perfect examples as could be found in 1989 in western Minnesota (see Plates 36 and 44). The proportions of the elements of the elevation (the straight-on, flat, drawing-board view) may be assessed in this view of the south side of the house. The length of the kitchen L is about equal to the width of the living room L. The proportions of the room volumes, the repetition of the window and gable shapes, the position of the porches, and the unity of the whole are characteristics of this house that could be identified in many variations in other L-houses.   This house has disappeared—probably burned—and its site has been filled in and graded flat. Chippewa County

PLATE 35. THE LARGEST BEDROOM on the second floor (of the house pictured in Plates 33 and 34) presents unexpected elegance. It is a simple room built under the gable roof in perfect bilateral symmetry around an axis pointed directly at the sunlight, so the radiance of the light follows the sight lines of the room. The use of space is essentially utilitarian, employing sloping ceilings, low side walls, and windows only in the south wall. No dormers were cut into the sloping planes of the roof. The stately formality of the window moldings and the capital-like corner blocks are reminiscent of the motifs of neo-classical architecture, which are usually not found in Minnesota L-houses. Chippewa County

PLATE 36.   A RARE CLASSIC L-HOUSE IN ALMOST ORIGINAL CONDITION (it may have had four- or eight-pane windows when it was built) still stands on the prairie with its back to the remaining north-south leg of its shelterbelt and its kitchen porch basking in the morning sunshine. There is enough paint remaining on the house to indicate how bright some farmhouses used to look, and how thoroughly evolved and successfully established they appeared, considering that only thirty years before the land had been occupied almost exclusively by the Native Americans. Yellow Medicine County

PLATE 37.   A FEW OLD KITCHEN PORCHES retain their sense of interplay with the light of the
prairie environment, although here it is a swarm of prairie grasses and flowers instead of a farmer that cross
the porch. The elaborate porch structure and decoration suggest that the hand of the craftsman was at work
here, but that hand did not actually form these parts, it only assembled them. No living room door opens
onto this kitchen porch; instead a formal front door and front porch were built on the south end of the
house, facing the county road. Yellow Medicine County

PLATE 38.   A THREE-QUARTER VIEW (of the house in Plates 36 and 37) shows how the porches contribute to the unified appearance of the house by introducing lines and planes of transition between the house roof and the ground. Without the porches, there would be only high, nearly blank walls between the roof and the ground, and there would be no fine detail or intricate rhythm in the composition of the house as a whole. The lines of the porch roofs tend to continue the lines of the gables and bring them down toward the ground, which creates the vague impression that a pyramid has been imposed upon the two upright boxes that form the main house. The porch roofs also shade the windows and doors under them and create darkened regions that give the first floor a somewhat heavier look, as though the porches were part of a broadened base of support for the second floor. Yellow Medicine County

PLATE 39.   EXCEPT FOR THE somewhat disproportionately large bay window, this is a classic L-house that has its design elements clustered around the living room L in a moderately well-balanced composition. As is virtually always the case, however, it is not a perfectly complete example, because several otherwise typical features are not present. Neither porch has lathe-turned Gothic posts, and there is no living room door to the kitchen porch. The two porches were not used in the usual fashion, because the house is turned so the kitchen porch faces south toward the township road when it would typically face the driveway. Here the formal front of the house and the front door face the driveway instead of facing the township road, with the result that the formal front door provided a more convenient route to the barnyard than did the kitchen door. Redwood County

PLATE 40. VIRTUALLY ALL THE ORIGINAL PRAIRIE has been plowed and cultivated by farmers who planted trees to protect their farmsteads from the wind. Those shelterbelts now appear to be islands of forest in a sea of cultivation. This view is from the northeast, so the house and barnyard appear to be in front, and toward the left end of the shelterbelt, which was planted along the west and north sides of the farmstead. Yellow Medicine County

PLATE 41. THE SIMPLE, GABLE-ROOFED rectangular shed was the basic unit of construction for most prairie architecture. Here there are five small plain sheds, a house that appears to be two sheds side by side, a barn formed by adding lean-tos on either side of a big shed, and a medium-sized granary shed with a very little shed on its roof as a ventilator. The masonry silo is the only exception to the use of shed construction, but it was built in the twentieth century, perhaps forty or fifty years after the wooden structures were built. Yellow Medicine County

PLATE 42. ALL THE BUILDINGS OF AN IDEAL BARNYARD front onto the perimeter of a 150-foot square piece of land lying across the top of a gentle hill. Here the structures are, from left to right, supply shed, windmill, hand pumps, barn, hoghouse, corncrib, granary, and henhouse. The machine shop is hidden behind the henhouse, and a garage is out of the picture to the right. This barnyard is larger than most at about 170 x 180 feet and contains two more buildings than average. The granary is unusually large and complex, having one bin underneath, four bins on the first floor, and five bins on the second floor. There are also lean-tos built onto the west and north sides of the granary to shelter machinery. In this arrangement the well is nearly at an equal distance from the house or each building, although it is, appropriately enough, closer to the barn and the hog house. Yellow Medicine County

PLATE 43. THE L-HOUSE SERVING THIS FARM (Plate 42) has a somewhat boxy and bland appearance because it has no open porch and little distinction among its main shapes and volumes. The porch was enclosed using the same standard windows that appear on the rest of the house, making the porch wall seem monotonous and indistinguishable from the house walls. Yellow Medicine County

PLATE 44. ALMOST EVERYTHING ABOUT THIS HOUSE, including situation, dimensions, and decoration, is typical of the classic L-house with one glaring exception—it has no open kitchen porch. The kitchen and living room approximate the sixteen foot squares (fifteen feet on the inside) that characterize L-houses. Instead of a classic open kitchen porch there was a somewhat ramshackle closed porch, inconsistent with the well-defined shapes and decoration of the rest of the house. The dimensions of the house are indicated in the floor plan illustration on page 29. This house is also pictured in Plates 45 and 46.
Yellow Medicine County

PLATE 45. THE VIEW FROM THE KITCHEN toward the living room includes, from left to right, the front kitchen window, the door to the porch, the living room, the stairway to the bedrooms, the back bedroom, and the back kitchen window. The stove and sink were behind the camera in this view. The three doorways in a row in the wall between the kitchen L and the living room L are typical of L-house design and join the three basic spaces of the house—the kitchen, the living room, and the bedrooms. The low ceilings and deliberate doorways between definitive blocks of space give this interior the compact clarity of purpose which was generally sought by L-house builders. The door and window moldings are of the same design in all three rooms on the ground floor, which is not usually the case in the common L-house. Yellow Medicine County

PLATE 46. THE BACK VIEW OF AN L-HOUSE often shows the house to be T-shaped because the living room segment extends beyond the back wall of the kitchen. Usually there are fewer windows in the back of the house, especially when it is to the north, as is the case here. There are four windows on the north end of the living room L like those on the other side facing south. This appears to be the result of a design principle rather than a response to a need for light. The bottom pair of windows open into the bedroom behind the living room as does the left window in the front, giving that room three full-sized windows while the kitchen has only one full-sized window and a smaller one. Water off the west-facing roof runs through drain-pipes that cross five walls, and changes direction ten times on its way to the cistern buried near the east end of the house. Yellow Medicine County

PLATE 47.   THE VIEW FROM THE NORTHWEST shows this house to be very similar to the house in Plate 46. However, the north wall of the kitchen and the north end of the living room L are in one continuous plane here, whereas the living room L extends beyond the north wall of the kitchen in the house of Plate 46. This house is L-shaped, while the house of Plate 46 is T-shaped. Lac qui Parle County

PLATE 48.   THE WIDE FRONT PORCH AND LARGE GABLE ABOVE IT give the west end of this house (also pictured in Plates 47, 49, and 50) a thoroughly developed appearance. The porch is an exception from the ideal type, which employed Gothic posts with brackets and railings. Here there are slim, smooth Roman columns with no brackets at the roof or railings around the perimeter of the floor. The full-sized gable above the porch gives the front of the house a more vertically pointed look than did the more common small gable or the absence of any gable at all. The four main gables employ the same decoration, and each has a pair of windows under it. From the front it looks as though the house may be cross-formed, but the roof ridge of the front gable is not continuous with the roof ridge of the kitchen L. Lightning rods stand atop three of the four main gables. Lac Qui Parle County

PLATE 49.   IN LATE WINTER AND EARLY SPRING, bright sunny days start drying the fields, and
fleecy clouds tend to erase the memory of the more dreary strains of winter, replacing them with an eager
and optimistic anticipation of spring planting. Today most farmers practice a shallow sort of rough tillage that
leaves the roots and stalks of last year's crop lying near the surface and only partially broken up. Nineteenth-
century farmers practiced moderately deep plowing (in special instances very deep subsoil plowing) followed
by rather thorough surface cultivation, primarily to keep the weeds down. The resulting crops grew quite
vigorously but the pulverized soil was vulnerable to erosion. The present system depends upon herbicides to
control the weeds, leaving the fields somewhat more resistant to erosion. Lac qui Parle County

PLATE 50. BASEMENTS WERE PRIMARILY ROOT CELLARS that might extend across the width of one segment of the house but not be dug out under the entire house. Their fieldstone walls were often constructed with larger stones toward the bottom and smaller ones near the top. An electric generator driven by a gasoline engine stands near the door. The pipe through the wall carried the exhaust outside. The broken up storage batteries lying on the floor could power a few lightbulbs when the generator was not running. The figure standing at the entrance is a cream separator. Lac qui Parle County

PLATE 51. LONG L-HOUSES typically have two rooms in their kitchen L segments rather than only one. Characteristically their kitchen chimneys stand about two-thirds of the way across the roof ridge of the kitchen L, and they have long kitchen porches (see also Plates 53, 54, and 56). This kitchen porch opened toward the barn-yard to the northwest, which allowed it to receive no morning light, and its function as a transition zone between the indoors and the outdoors was nullified by allowing no doors to open onto it. The porch roof was supported by smooth Roman columns rather than the more common Gothic posts. Apparently the danger of lightning was considered to be serious because the house was fitted with five lightning rods rather than the usual two or three. This house is now gone, and there is nothing to be seen here except a plowed field. Yellow Medicine County

PLATE 52. THE FORMAL COMPOSITION OF THIS HOUSE appears to be the product of one mind, as does the unusually sophisticated decoration. The porch is missing, but it was probably a flat-topped balcony porch judging from the unpainted area on the wall and the tall slender door that opened onto its roof. The relatively wide-angled gables contain lace-like decoration of an especially delicate and complex sort. The gable wall is decorated with patterns of fish scale, diamond and three-edged shingles. Entablatures with precise rows of little cubes under them were placed over the windows and doors. The little cubes were reiterated in the simulated capitals between the gable ends and the corner moldings, and under the eaves of the bay-window roof. This house has now disappeared. Yellow Medicine County

PLATE 53. THIS HOUSE IS A REPRESENTATIVE LONG L-house with a standard living-room L containing a living-room, and a back bedroom. The typical kitchen L consists of a back kitchen and a kitchen-dining room. On the second floor there are four bedrooms each of the same size as the room immediately below it. The chimneys are in typical positions for a long L-house, and so are the doors, although two are hidden in this view. The living room door is under the foot of the L-shaped porch roof (left). The kitchen-dining room door is out of sight behind the corner of the enclosed portion of the porch, and the kitchen door is within the enclosed portion of the porch. (See Plate 54 for a similar long L-house porch with three doors opening onto it). The foundation does not rise much above ground level so the house appears to be sitting right down in the grass. Yellow Medicine County

PLATE 54. FROM THE SOUTHEAST THIS PORCH may be seen for the social crossroads that it was before the wheat and wild grasses filled up the yard. Living room, dining room, and kitchen all opened onto the long (about twenty-four feet) kitchen porch as though each was an independent compartment of the house, although they were all connected to each other inside. The sunburst decorations in the gables above the porch and on the east end are unusual as are the boxed eaves which appear on the kitchen-L roof, but not on the living room L roof. The chimneys and lightning rods are in typical positions, but there appear to be no rain gutters. This porch was screened-in subsequent to its construction, and the framework has muddled up the look of purity possessed by the Gothic porch posts. Swift County

PLATE 55.   SINCE THE KITCHEN L WAS QUITE LONG, about twenty-four feet, it usually contained two upstairs bedrooms, but as there was no room for a hallway, one had to go through the first bedroom to reach the second one. In some cases a second staircase was built in the back of the kitchen to serve the end bedroom. The uniform distribution of windows and doors on this side of the house give it a trim and orderly look except for the blank area on the far end of the long L. That end looks like an addition to the original design, but the kitchen chimney comes down outside the wall that separates the kitchen-dining room from the back kitchen. If that wall was originally an outside wall, the chimney would have been built inside it, which implies that the long L was part of the original structure and not an addition. Lac qui Parle County

PLATE 56. MOST L-HOUSES LOOK RATHER PLAIN AND DULL as though they were assembled mechanically without the application of much craft or inspiration—you sense the mindless replication of the machine. However a small number (under 10 percent), have their own sculptural and architectonic vigor. Here the interpenetrating roof planes, detailed dormer and bay windows, and extensive porch decoration suggest that extraordinary effort went into the design. The porch is L-shaped, although barely so. The roof turn required building an additional valley and ridge, adding a post, and extending the porch floor and footings—a good deal of extra effort and cost for little practical gain. Unpainted silhouettes on the walls where the engaged Gothic half-posts once stood and marks under the porch roof from a row of spindles indicate that the original porch was detailed and decorated. Yellow Medicine County

PLATE 57. LONG L-HOUSES HAVE A LINEAR ASPECT because their three main rooms are built in a row. When their doors are open, as they are here, you can look straight through all three of them. A sense of interaction with the outdoors is usually not strong in L-houses, but here the bay window projects out from the room rather far, so one feels partly surrounded by the world outdoors when one stands in it. The living room door (center) opens onto the porch. It provides almost no sense of transition between the indoor and outdoor light and space. Nothing about it suggests that the whole outside world is the other side. It has no vestibule, no coat closet, no windows; it could as well be a closet door. Yellow Medicine County

PLATE 58.   USUALLY THE NATURAL DECAY of an abandoned farmhouse proceeds with some uniformity, but here the south side of the room—the weather side—has begun to disintegrate while the north half looks as if it had been lived in quite recently. When the shingles on the roof failed, water got in and rotted the roof and the rafters, which allowed the ceiling and a portion of the inside wall and wallpaper to fall to the floor. That wreckage is composed of stark value contrasts, straight lines, hard edges, and violent diagonals of a masculine nature compared to the feminine appearance of the north side of the room with its lighter more uniform values, its flowered wallpaper, and its curving, diaphanous curtains. This Plate and Plate 57 are interior views of the house pictured in Plate 56. Big Stone County

PLATE 59. THIS COMPOUND L-HOUSE retained much of its original character intact until it disappeared in 1993. Usually the smaller details and finer textures of L-houses were replaced by successive modernizing owners or lost to the weather and vandals after the houses were abandoned. Here the multifaceted vitality of the original house could be sensed in the porch posts, kitchen porch screens, wooden roof shingles, and original eight-pane windows. Lac qui Parle County

PLATE 60. AS IT NOW STANDS, this large two-story house is somewhat stark and plain, with vast uninterrupted roof surfaces and wall planes. It has something of a barracks or dormitory look to it in this view—an impression reinforced by its having five bedrooms upstairs. The wings are each sixteen and a half feet wide by eighteen feet long and the center section is sixteen and a half feet wide by twenty-four and a half feet deep, so the extreme dimensions of the house, not counting the back porch, are twenty-four and a half by fifty-two and a half feet. This side of the house is symmetrical except that there are two upstairs windows on the left wing and only one on the right wing. The center section does not project very much, and there is no bay window to articulate this face of the house. The two porches added some detail and variation. Lac qui Parle County

PLATE 61. THIS DRIVEWAY PASSES AN UPPER BARNYARD on the left and an unusually expansive houseyard on the right. Then it continues to the end of the barnyard where it turns into a field road. There is a sort of plateau that forms the upper yard level, which was mostly an area for human activities while everything over the edge of the plateau was devoted to field activities or animal concerns. The bank barn was built into the edge of that plateau so that the main floor of the barn could admit vehicles driven up a low ramp and through a pair of large double doors, while the ground level of the barn had smaller doorways for the animals. Lac qui Parle County

PLATE 62. THIS FARMSTEAD WITH ITS LARGE HOUSE, two barns, and tall windmill appears to have had a vigorous and productive history. The driveway comes in from the west and goes through the shelterbelt and barnyard before it reaches the house. The more common arrangement would have had the barnyard to the east and downwind from the house, and the driveway would have passed the house on its way to the barnyard. The large cottonwoods in the shelterbelt suggest that it is quite old because cottonwoods have not been planted much since the 1920s. The farm seems to have grown over the years since it has two barns, and both of them were expanded by adding lean-tos on the sides and ends. The field in the foreground has lost much of its original black topsoil and lighter colored subsoil now appears at the surface forming mud-crack patterns. Lac qui Parle County

PLATE 63.   THE SUN BATHES THE FRONT SIDE OF THE HOUSE from the farmstead of Plate 62, across its fenced-in yard. Its overall design is an uneasy amalgam of an inner L-house with an outer facade that obscures the distinctions between the working volumes of the inner house. The two porches and the four-window bays extend in a horizontal band of shapes. Their roofs are connected to form a continuous plane that seems to cut into the central projection of the dining-room segment of the house. That implied penetration, the lack of vertical moldings on the bay window, the absence of upward-pointing dormer gables on the roof, and the use of short posts that do not meet the porch roof—all tend to hold the house down, visually speaking, and resist any sense of vertical movement or upward growth. Lac qui Parle County

PLATE 64.   IT IS STILL POSSIBLE TO IMAGINE this, kitchen from within the house of Plate 63, as it was in the past when it would have had a large table at which to feed a dozen or more workers and family members during the wheat harvest. Professor Fred W. Peterson says in his *Homes in the Heartland* that this was a farm of 470 acres owned and worked by a large and socially active family. Through the doorway to the right was a large dining room, and behind this room was a back kitchen (almost as large as this one) that contained the stove and sink. It was served in turn by a pantry, the stairs to the cellar, and a small back porch at the back door. In the backyard there stood a small summer kitchen (not common in the midwest) where additional cooking could be done.
Lac qui Parle County

PLATE 65. TAKING ADVANTAGE OF AN ELEVATED SITE, this farmstead house is located on top of the hill. The bank barn is built into the edge of the hill so the barn has a second-floor entrance on the west side facing the house. Two other entrances are on the ground floor to provide easy access, possibly to a herd of milk cows. Since a hay wagon could be driven into the second-floor hayloft (see also Plate 61), no large hay door was built under the roof peak of this end of the barn. The trees to the left of the house are in the north-south limb of the shelterbelt. Those behind the barn are in the east-west part but they are actually on the other side of the township road, so the two sections do not join at the corner behind the house. The house, barn, and shelterbelt have now all disappeared. Lac qui Parle County

PLATE 66.   SOME OF THE TWO-WING HOUSE DESIGNS that evolved out of the L-house approach exhibited shifting and unresolved aesthetic values. The beveling of the corners of the living-dining-room projection and the placing of windows in the resulting angled planes made the center section appear to radiate outward like a giant bay window. The beveling of the corners also produced a series of design repercussions that were antithetical to the simple structural clarity of the L-house. The suspended roof corners are the single most distinctive parts of the house, but they are not satisfying because they are too close to the tops of the windows, and their means of support is unclear. The implication of structural support is made by the moldings over the joints, between the beveled sections, and the front face of the center section. Lac qui Parle County

PLATE 67. CUBE HOUSES, like this one, were the second-most common type of farmhouse, after L-houses, built in western Minnesota in the classic period from 1863 to 1893. They became even more prominent between 1893 and 1912 when farming authorities were recommending them and more farmers had saved the money to build a full-sized house all at once. The essential cube house had a square floor plan about twenty-five to twenty-eight feet on a side, was always two stories tall, and was topped with a truncated pyramid roof with one or more large gables. The joining of the cube and pyramid shapes created a volume that contained the maximum number of cubic feet of interior space per square foot of exterior wall and roof area, which minimized both the amount of material needed for construction and heat loss. Lac Qui Parle County

PLATE 68. THE FIELDS IN WINTER usually carry no greater depth of snow than this, but when the house was near the center of the property at the end of a long driveway, it created some sense of isolation from the neighbors and from the roads to town. If the snow became deeper than this, a sleigh would run easier than a wagon or carriage. Driving to town was done less often in winter, but the route might be shorter because the sleigh could be taken overland across the frozen fields and meadows. Lac qui Parle County

PLATE 69. SCHOOLHOUSES employed the same construction methods used for small farmhouses. They were simple structures, modest in size, and each was a little different from the other. The gable-roofed, rectangular shed shape was at the core of the design, with appurtenances added to suit the situation. This one is a single-story structure with standard-sized windows on each side, and a stove and chimney at the center of the end. The identifier of the schoolhouse was the little bell tower, present here on the left end of the roof ridge, although many classic rural schoolhouses never had one, so the teacher resorted to the hand-held bell. This school acquired a front-porch extension sometime after its original construction to contain the bustle of the coming and going of numerous children and probably to provide a coat room. Yellow Medicine County

PLATE 70. SOME OF THE COUNTRY CHURCHES had fine, satisfying proportions and crisp discreet lines and edges. Here the door and window shapes, all with Gothic arches, are subtly arranged to provide a feeling of both stable centrality and lift. Most of the churches were Lutheran. Like the farmhouses there are no two churches exactly alike, and most of them have been altered since their original construction. Many have had wide porches built onto their fronts. That has thrown their proportions out of balance and interfered with the uninterrupted visual rise of the tower. This church has not been altered, so the original structure still rises with the humble grace and propriety that generally characterized the people's faith. Yellow Medicine County

PLATE 71. MOST FARM FAMILY MEMBERS were laid to rest in modest cemeteries next to their churches. Some cemeteries were established on relatively high isolated places with long views out across the prairie. There were only a few family cemeteries such as this one, which is now surrounded by a plowed field. The large stone was placed in 1884. The smallest stones mark the graves of children who died very young and were only able to make this small mark on the fertile prairie. Big Stone County

Design: Barbara J. Arney

Typeface: Bembo

Photograph Reproduction: 200 line screen
Pantone 457/Black/Black Tritones

Prepress: Encore Color Group
Eagan, Minnesota